ASK OTHERS, TRUST YOURSELF

The Entrepreneurial Woman's Key to Success

Congratulations on your completion of
the WBC Business Coaching Program
www.canisius.edu/wbc

888-8280

Canisius
COLLEGE

Disclaimer

This Book is designed to provide general educational information about the subject matter covered. It should not be construed as legal, accounting or other professional advice. If legal or other expert assistance is required, the services of a competent professional should be sought.

It is not the purpose of this Book to reprint all the information that is otherwise available to business owners and aspiring entrepreneurs, but to encourage and inspire. The client situations described are composites and/or fictionalizations of actual case studies in order to preserve the privacy and confidentiality of the author's actual clients. The author shall have neither liability nor responsibility to any person or entity with respect to any loss or damage caused or alleged to be caused directly or indirectly by the information contained in this Book.

Booklocker.com, Inc.
2009

ASK OTHERS, TRUST YOURSELF

The Entrepreneurial Woman's Key to Success

Elisa Balabram

To my parents, Fany and Moysés Balabram, for their strength, wisdom, and inspiration.

Acknowledgments

This book wouldn't exist if it wasn't for a brainstorming session I had with my mentor Robert J. Lee. Thank you! I would also like to thank Débora Balabram, Jill Kanter, Allison Lehr, Maria Li and Eileen S. Winterble for their constant cheerleading and encouragement. Special thanks to my colleagues who reviewed the book and offered very constructive feedback: Vaidila Kungys and Jennifer Ruskin. To Renata Moreira Marquez, a heartfelt thanks for the cover artwork. Thank you to the editors Amy Tannembaum and Judy G., and to Priscilla Stephan for all the referrals. And thanks to Nina L. Kaufman, Patrick J. MacKrell, Karen Watt and Michael Wilhite for their comments and feedback. For the support and spiritual guidance, I thank Marli M. L. Chaves and Robert Baker. For kindly sharing her PR and marketing expertise in promoting the book, I thank Kristin Marquet.

Thanks to all my mentors, family and friends who are always there for me and ready to cheer me on each step of the way. And thank you to all my clients for their inspiration and will to pursue their dreams no matter what.

Table of Contents

Introduction

I've always encouraged people to pursue their business dreams. Actually, it took me some time to accept the fact that some people never thought of the possibility of being an entrepreneur or could be overwhelmed by the thought of starting their own business, and may prefer to work for somebody else. Since you are reading this book, you are already pursuing your entrepreneurial goals or at least getting closer to making it happen. Congratulations! As you know from experience, running a business is challenging but amazingly rewarding. Being a small business owner can be lonely sometimes, but it doesn't have to be.

The idea for this book came to me after years editing my e-magazine, WomenandBiz.com, working at not-for-profit economic development organizations and offering business assistance to women. I soon realized that many women, when starting their businesses, had little or no clue about the types of business assistance available to them, or even that they could ask for help. This book is for those women who are about to start a business, or have been in business for one day or many years, and want to make sure their business succeeds. I will share my experience as a woman running my business, interviewing female business owners, helping to build my family's business, as well as my years of experience coaching other women about running theirs. My original plan was to prepare a directory of the associations and organizations that provide free or low-cost services to women, but the idea grew into this more complete guide. Not only is it important to know where to go, it is important to ask crucial questions, to work with professionals you trust, to have a support group, and to know when to pursue the suggestions you receive. You will learn more about who you are and you will have the tools you need to listen to your intuition and trust yourself.

This book will explain how you can ask for help without feeling powerless. Your strength in fact will allow you to realize that not having all the answers is okay. Asking for help takes courage and wisdom. You need courage to admit to yourself and others that you don't have all the answers. You need wisdom to decide which actions to take. You have to be prepared to accept or refuse the advice you receive, and to discern what works and what doesn't. You might be asking, "If I don't know the answer, how do I know which advice to follow?" That's a perfectly valid question, and I will address that in this book as well.

You will also learn when the best time is to ask for help. Yes, you guessed it... NOW! You might be thinking, "Why would I ask for help, especially now?" There is always a case to be made for asking for help. If your business is thriving and growing, it might be time to review your strategies and to ensure that business growth continues; if you have reached a plateau, it might be time to reinvent yourself; if you are in a lot of debt, it might be time to re-evaluate your approach. No matter what your situation, asking questions can help you get at least one step closer to your goal.

This book will show you what questions to ask and, most important, how to listen. After coaching many female business owners, I've realized that often they don't even know that their issues reach beyond what they originally thought. These lessons will help you to stay open to the variety of questions that might be raised by your coach; he/she will make sure you are covering all the loose ends.

I will also provide you with specific questions to ask the professionals you might need to consult with as you grow. Finally, I offer you a list of resources that can help you take the next step.

CHAPTER 1

Self-Inquiry

Before you think about asking for help, I invite you to do a self-inquiry. Through questions and self-awareness, you will learn to investigate and examine your own feelings and intuition. There are probably more answers within you that can help you succeed than you'll find in any book, from any expert, or through any other resource.

It might be that you have only thought about launching a business, or it might be that you already have a business but envision making millions of dollars and you are stuck. There is nothing wrong with either picture, but it's important to find out where you stand and to think about your goals. Do you want to make a living, or do you want to thrive and succeed beyond that point? Is the purpose of the business to change the world?

Would you like to be able to retire early? Do you want to keep working on your business forever?

There are no right or wrong answers, and even when you figure out what you really want at this point, your opinions and needs may change down the road. The business environment may change, as the market changes, your clients might want different things, and the competition might get fierce. When competitors take a large portion of your market, you can't keep doing what you've always done. On the other hand your lifestyle, priorities and family needs may change as well. When your family grows or your parents age, they will require more of your time, and you might need to readjust.

Here are some self-inquiry questions I found useful when working with women business owners. You might have thought of them before, but take some time to check in again, and see if your answers have changed.

- What is my vision for this business a year from now; two years from now; five, ten years from now?
- What is my vision for my life and my family's life?

Are the two previous visions aligned? If they are, great! If not, which one could you revise to satisfy your needs and wants?

- How do I feel about my business today? Is it everything I dreamed of or is it draining me?
- What is my life's purpose? Is this business aligned with it? Or would this business help me fulfill my life's purpose by providing me the financial security I need to pursue it?
- How happy am I to work on this business? Would I rather be doing something else?
- Would it be fine to work 24/7? Or would I rather create a business that gives me the flexibility to only work part-time?
- Do I want to keep control of my business? Or would I like to have partners and share the responsibilities and profits?
- Would I like to build it, and then sell it in a few years?

Feel free to add your own questions.

Reasons you started your business (T or F)

T ☐   F ☐   I wanted to create a job for myself and make a
living.
T ☐   F ☐   I wanted to generate extra income while still
keeping my full time job.
T ☐   F ☐   I wanted to be my own boss and never have to work
for anybody else again.
T ☐   F ☐   I'm going to give this business a try, but if it doesn't
work, the doors are still open at my last job.
T ☐   F ☐   I want to have unlimited money coming in, and live
an abundant and prosperous life always.
T ☐   F ☐   This business allows me to practice all my talents
and creativity.

The above statements will help you learn more about yourself,
your commitment to your business, and your intentions.

Keep your answers handy; they will be helpful when you
need to make crucial business decisions. You can always ask for
help before reaching final conclusions to the questions above.
But by looking at the big picture, you will know the level of
help you need.

If you have no idea of your vision, describe your ideal day, and what it would look like. Or look for signs in your current life. When do you feel the most alive? What do you enjoy most about your average day? The clearer you can get about your vision, the better and easier it is to build your business and get where you want to go.

Being True to Yourself

While dealing with the self-inquiry process, make sure to use a method that works for you. When a friend of mine had to choose between a new job offer and a growth opportunity at his current job, I suggested that he find a quiet place to reflect on it, to meditate and listen to the voice within. How he would do that, and which meditation strategy he would use, was ultimately up to him. Later, he told me that the meditation gave him a clearer sense of the best course of action. As long as you don't resist the process, allow yourself to learn on your own terms, and give yourself the freedom to choose what's best and move forward when you are ready, you will be able to find the method of self-inquiry that helps you achieve your goals. The book *The Seeker's Guide: Making Your Life a Spiritual*

Adventure, by Elizabeth Lesser, offers many meditation techniques to help you get started, or go deeper with your current meditation practice. (This is also an excellent book for anyone seeking spiritual growth).

Since I've been writing, I read about other writers' methods of writing. Some people write until they reach 1,000 words each day, others first think about what they are going to write for days before writing, others write until they reach two pages a day, and still others prepare folders for each chapter and fill them with their research before starting to write.

We are all unique individuals with our own personalities, histories, and ways of being. When faced with many options, some people give each method a try to see what works best for them. Some people like to wait and look for signs. If they hear about the same system again and again, they pursue it. Others are willing to invest head on without being sure of the consequences, and some will do nothing. Which one are you? As long as you are not prone to doing nothing, you will be able to move forward, even if a method you try doesn't lead anywhere.

In the discovery process, patience is important. It might take a while until you can see tangible results in your business, and going back and forth trying different strategies might not help either. You can choose to stick to a method for six months, and then reassess the situation. But if the method is not working for you, or the business is getting worse with no signs of improvement, it might be best to change your strategy immediately.

Through the process of self-inquiry, make sure to be kind to yourself. Running your own business can be lonely, and there isn't much recognition. I recommend that you take the time to celebrate every discovery, every deal, every success, every challenge you overcome, every opportunity. Don't wait for others to notice how great you are. You are great now, as you are—acknowledge it.

Inner Wisdom

Your inner wisdom is an undeniably strong source of inspiration. It doesn't matter where you're from, what your background is or what education you have. Inner wisdom can be very strong, and everyone has it. It might take a while to uncover it, or to use it to its full potential, but it can be done.

When making a crucial decision, check in with yourself. See how the course of action you choose resonates with you. Ask yourself and ask somebody else. Even do a little research and investigation on your own, to make sure that the advice you are receiving is accurate. If it still makes sense, then go for it. Do not allow yourself to be caught up in the hype of someone telling you how wonderful things can be, and make a quick decision to follow their advice. Otherwise you might forget to take a few minutes to look inside yourself and figure out if this is the right path.

Here are a few ways to find answers from within. Find a quiet place to meditate, sit down and relax, keep your feet flat on the ground to remain grounded and alert. Take a few deep breaths and concentrate on inhaling and exhaling. Then think about the situation you are facing, and ask yourself one or a few of these questions:

- What is the real problem?
- How can I best solve this issue?

- What is the best option for me?
- Who should I consult with, if anyone?
- How do any of these options move me closer to my goals?

To deal with tough questions, you may also consider journaling, creating a vision board, drawing, taking your mind off the situation or visualizing solutions for the issues you are facing. With journaling, vision boards and drawing you can work on what comes to mind without censoring yourself or thinking too much about whether it makes sense. After you're done—sometimes it takes a few days to complete this step— you can review what you've done and look for signs of what you consider the most important step to follow. If for any reason you were not satisfied with the writing you did, you can pick up from where you left off and continue at another time. Eventually your ego stays quiet and your true self will show you the way. Other options include taking your mind off the situation, by singing, exercising, practicing yoga or dancing. Doing these things may help you clear your mind, and may allow you to be open to receiving an "A-HA" moment. Visualizing allows you to focus on what you want to create.

Make sure to take your time, so that you don't end up focusing on what you don't want.

The method you use depends on your personality, and if you have no idea which one is best for you, that might be the first question you need to ask yourself. "Would I like to journal about this situation? Would I like to create a vision board? Would I like to draw?" You also need to be brave to read what you wrote, to interpret your drawings, to see beyond the pictures you chose for your vision board. You could ask someone else to tell you what he or she sees on your vision board or drawing, since his or her perception can be enlightening.

If you are able to take a few minutes a day to connect with your heart and intuition, the answers you are seeking might come to you. What are you feeling that could make a difference in your business right now? Don't get discouraged if the answers don't come to you the first time you try. That happens. I suggest that you change the question to an easier one, and pursue answers to that question first as a way to practice.

You can concentrate on just one issue, or you can explore different issues. Usually I choose one issue that I'm having problems with. I start exploring the surface of the issue, but as I continue to journal or draw or use any other strategy, I end up going deeper and deeper into the problem and the final question and answer, even though it might not be the one that I first envisioned, will bring me the inspiration I need.

Can you ever get the wrong answers? Of course! If you are not in tune with your inner self, your internal voices will keep trying to protect you and will try anything possible to prevent a change in the status quo, or to make you avoid "mistakes". The answers you receive from within might not actually be the wrong answers; they might be the answers you are ready to face at this time. By focusing your attention in how you feel about the answers that are coming up, you will start noticing if there is any resistance to them and/or if they are the "wrong" answers for you to pursue. Stay true to your needs and be kind to yourself. Don't beat yourself up if you choose not to follow your intuition, or if you ignore the signs and decide to face deeper issues in the future. The energy spent blaming yourself could be used instead to take corrective action and make better decisions in the future, by learning to better understand and follow your intuition.

No method is bulletproof. Therefore, the more you research, the more people you trust and talk to, the more you listen to your inner wisdom, the more likely you will be directed to your best option at the moment. The most important thing is to take action. If you just think about your issues without doing anything, your ego, or other voices inside of you, might take over, dominate the conversation, and stop you from taking a real step forward.

Deciding to take action is not easy, but similar to working with a therapist, discussing the issues is just the first step. After seeing a therapist you have to take action with the new insights you've received, and live a different way, try different things in order to feel the changes. Remember to keep this in mind when asking for business help too. You are responsible for your own business growth, you are not handing the success and destiny of your business to anyone else. It is always up to you to get things done, even if getting things done means hiring someone who knows how to do it. It is still your decision to hire a skilled professional. Remember to trust yourself at all times and to take action.

Knowing Yourself

Once you know in your core that you are in charge of your life and business, and nobody else can influence how you feel or act without your consent, you will be better prepared to receive the help you need. How do you get to that mindset? By keeping the focus within yourself. You can learn breathing exercises, you can meditate, and you can follow the self-inquiry exercises discussed earlier in this chapter.

As your business grows and you yourself are changing and facing different challenges, or going deeper within yourself in order to learn, the questions will change. Be open to asking yourself different, and more specific questions, such as these ones suggested by one of my mentors, the consultant Karen Watt, MA:

- If you are not feeling peaceful/joyful or when challenging feelings arise, what are your feelings trying to tell you?
- How often do you feel this way?

- What is the pattern you keep recreating and why?
- What are your behaviors that are contributing to the pattern?
- If you didn't act this way, how would you act differently?
- What would happen if everything remained the same? How would you feel?
- What change in behavior would give you a different result or change how you feel about the situation?
- What can you do today to start changing the way you think about the situation and the way you act?
- What specific steps can you take?

Ms. Watt also suggests that when stuck or when you need to go deeper, different questions might be more appropriate:

- What is the question you are avoiding asking yourself?
- What question would deepen your understanding of the situation?
- How can you live with the question and tolerate the ambiguity of not knowing the answer immediately to garner the full understanding of the situation?

Take some time to ask yourself these questions, and be open to what may come up. You might not want to face your patterns and own ways to handle pressure, but once you know they exist, it is your choice to continue your behavior or to make a change that can improve your life. Even if you don't see any issues with your own patterns, by consciously focusing on yourself and on how you act in certain situations, you will be able to move forward and to become the best you can be.

One of the advantages of becoming more knowledgeable of who you are, and of your triggers, is that you become aware of having certain reactions to your coach or mentor.

- If you feel the need always to be right every time someone disagrees with you, or has a different opinion about your next step, you might feel threatened and angry, and might miss out on a great business opportunity.
- If you feel the need to be loveable by agreeing with everyone, you might be ignoring your own feelings and intuition, and might end up doing something that isn't really true to yourself or your values and not so good for your business.

19

- If you are not sure of what you want or need, you might have a tendency to follow someone else's advice, without fully analyzing it.

To get a sense of your triggers or how you relate with others, ask yourself: How do I feel/act/behave in relation to other people? Being conscious of your style is only one step in this process. Since you've been behaving a certain way most of your life, it isn't easy to break this pattern. With effort and daily exercises you can become aware of the pattern so that you can act in a different way. If you are the person I described who needs to always be right, the next time someone disagrees with you, stop for a moment and realize that it's not a matter of right or wrong but a difference of opinion. This might prevent you from feeling so compelled to put your foot down and stop listening.

Visualization

You can use visualization techniques in all areas of your

business. Once you focus on finding the answers, the solutions, the key personnel, the funds—your results—will materialize effortlessly.

The answers to your business questions exist either within you, within someone you know, or within someone they know. One example of visualization might be to visualize someone who can help you. Even after searching for the right person, if you can't find anyone willing to help you, you can take a break from your search, just sit still, relax and visualize who the right person might be. You can focus your attention on the skill set and experience you're looking for. Continue to look and stay open to finding the right person. It might be that that one person who you didn't think of asking is the one with the answer for you. You will notice that the more you focus, the more quickly this person will show up for you.

As you develop your visualization skills, you will be able to manifest the results you need, or the person you need to help you with a particular project. For example, someone might just mention a project he/she worked on in the past, or someone new you meet at a networking event or trip might be able to help you. This is the alignment you are looking for and the universe will respond. In different times of my life, through visualization or trust, I manifested the exact person I needed to be in touch with. Don't forget that sometimes you might end up encountering some people who aren't the best fit, so it is critical to stay alert.

Things to remember before asking for help:

- Inquire within.
- Be honest and true to yourself.
- Listen to your inner wisdom.
- Journal, draw, create a vision board, and get clear about your intentions.
- Visualize the desired outcomes.
- Check in with yourself at all times.

CHAPTER 2

Why Would Anyone Ask for Help?
Why Would You?

Do you think you need to do it alone? Do you need to show that you have the passion and drive to get it done, no matter what others say or think of your idea? Are you under the impression that other business owners in the community are achieving success single-handedly?

Even if the answer to all these questions is yes, there is only so much one can do. Ask yourself this: Are you ready and willing to establish a successful and growing business? If so, then you must be willing to ask others for help.

You may know everything there is to know about your product or service, and you should. But what about your business, what about your market, what about your competitors, what about market trends, new technology, new markets, tax breaks, or new and unconventional ways to sell? The reality is that even if you decide to find out the answers to these questions by yourself, it might take a long time. In addition, you might not know which questions to ask. When you don't know that the government, for example, has incentives to support the development of new technology, it's not likely that that information will fall into your lap, is it? But if you create an advisory board, and if you join networking groups, attend events, or work with a coach, the information will pop up at some point and you will be thrilled that you sought help.

We always have to start from some point, learn from someone, somehow, before we can walk, talk, eat, cook, drive, or run a business on our own. I encourage my clients when on a budget, to first study whatever they are interested in on their own, but then ask for assistance as needed. For example, I taught myself how to design a website using HTML language, back in 1999, by reading the instructions that came with the software I purchased, by looking for free solutions online, and studying a lot. I did it! But when I uploaded the first site I ever designed, I panicked and called the customer support at my website's host. "Hey, I uploaded my website but the pictures are not coming up, how come???" And the answer was simple, "Well, you've got to upload the pictures in order to see them!" It was a little embarrassing, but I learned in a minute what could have taken me hours to figure out. Time is money, energy, and an opportunity to do other more creative and fun things. By calling and asking for help, I saved myself many headaches. Since then, I have learned a lot in the process of creating websites. However, every now and then, something new comes up, and instead of struggling for a few hours I pick up the phone and call someone who I know will have the answer right away.

Asking for business help can usually save you time and money. It can free up your time, so that you can take time to analyze your business, do some research or even get some rest. You can choose to research your industry at the local business library. Even better, some libraries offer free online chats with librarians, and you don't even need to leave your home as long as you have a library card. The business library is just one of the free resources you can use with your extra time.

To begin with, you might need help figuring out what you really want your business to be. Once a client who was originally thinking of starting a child care business but later changed her mind, came back to the office a few months later to ask how she could start a cleaning services business. I went back to the basics, and asked questions like, "Why do you want to start this business? What's your real passion, is this it? Have you thought of how much work is involved in starting and running this business? Are you willing to do the work?" (You could be your own coach and ask yourself those questions.)

I was concerned because she had a totally different business idea just a few months earlier. It turned out that she wasn't passionate about these business ideas at all, and after I pointed out the reality of running each business, and we discussed her passions, she decided to pursue her real dream and go back to school to pursue a career in health, even though it would take years to get the degree. Therefore, I recommend that you think seriously about these questions and consult with more than one person, while always asking yourself what you really want.

By listening to what others have to say about your business and business strategies you are opening yourself to a new world of possibilities. Your advisors might have been through similar situations and can help you skip certain steps that might eventually harm your business. They could show you how to increase sales without increasing expenses, how to create new sales channels, or how to come up with a different product line that matches your mission and satisfies a need that you'd never thought of before. They can share information with you about grants that you might not otherwise discover. And they possibly can tell you how to obtain financing without paying a high interest rate.

Brainstorming

Sometimes when you are so involved in your business, and making sure you can make ends meet, you don't have the time or vision to see the big picture. You may emulate your peers, regardless of their success, because that is what you know, and that's how you learned to do things. However, there might be other ways to run your business, alternative ways to promote it, to manage it and to grow it. Of course, you can analyze your business yourself, but it might be hard for you to take a step back to identify the areas that need changing. Even if you can see the issues, it might be difficult for you to come up with solutions.

To ensure that you are aware of alternative approaches, here are a few questions you could ask yourself, or your mastermind group or coach (for more information on mastermind groups and coaches, read chapter 3):

- What are other types of businesses I admire or consider successful?
- Could I apply their tools to my business? How could I do that?
- Would it be possible to create a new department?
- How effective would it be to pursue each new strategy?

Reflecting on those questions, and also brainstorming with a coach or support group about them, will help you to come up with creative ways to grow your business. For example, you might have been running a corner flower shop for years, and you understand that the business is seasonal, so you stay the same size. However, all of a sudden a new store opens across the street, or other online businesses start growing and taking your clientele. What can you do? You could do nothing, or you could brainstorm and come up with unique strategies.

When working with a coach, or brainstorming/consulting with your team, several new and creative ideas could come up during the meeting. Could you sell your flowers online? Probably yes, but would you prefer not to? Could you submit bids to sell flowers to government agencies? Could you create a flower membership card? Members could pay a monthly fee, for flowers with a few bonuses. Alternatively, you may choose to find a specific niche that the large companies simply can't serve. You can create flower arrangements for a specific occasion and a specific target audience and maybe even add inspirational phrases and wonderful handmade baskets that cannot be found elsewhere. Then, even those who buy online would still come to you for that special bouquet. You could eventually come up with these ideas and others on your own, but when you ask a coach for help, you can get additional support to think of creative concepts and an execution plan that will help you succeed.

Being Accountable

I've noticed that things are more likely to get accomplished when you make yourself accountable to taking action. I remember several years ago, when my online magazine for female business owners, WomenandBiz.com, was a mere idea. I shared it with a colleague of mine who was considering pursuing her own dreams of going back to theater, so I decided and committed to starting my online magazine, and she decided to taking acting classes. We shook on it and both of us followed through with our commitments just a few months later.

That's not to say that every time you have an idea you should tell the world. That's not the case at all, but having one or two (I had two) people holding you accountable for achieving your goal, can help keep you focused and motivated. I'd recommend having at least one person who you can talk to once a week, to share updates on your progress. Because even when life gets in the way, you will be motivated to find some time to at least take one step toward your ultimate goal.

You don't necessarily need to be working with a coach and a formal agreement; you could simply ask a friend/colleague/

mentor to check in with you every once in a while, in exchange for you doing the same for them. The difference with using a coach is that he or she might be able to help you brainstorm a business move that a friend might not have the knowledge to help you with. But still, a friend might be enough to keep you motivated and focused on the end result.

Managing Crisis

What I especially like about asking for help is that it can change your perspective on a situation. When things go wrong within your business, it can initially be difficult to see a solution. Instead, it is common to start creating negative thoughts based upon *should, could, would.* All one can feel is the drama of what went wrong.

A few months ago a client shared with me how frustrated and upset she was that a new product that she had sold had a problem. Her clients would realize it as soon as they opened the package, and she was worried about their reaction and how it could impact her business. During this stressful moment, she couldn't see the big picture or think of how to handle those customers. My position from the outside allowed me to be proactive. I said to her, "If you have the contact information of those clients, reach out to them immediately, apologize and let them know that you are willing to replace the product and even offer a free gift. If you can't reach them, instead of being afraid of receiving nasty calls, prepare a scripted response. For example, when someone is calling you in despair and being rude, you could change the dynamic by saying I'm so happy you called us, we were hoping you would. We identified the problem but didn't have a way to reach you. Here is what we can do for you.... It is not likely that they will still be upset, since you are offering them a solution." Of course some cases might be more difficult than others, but once you are prepared with a professional and kind response, the customer will most likely respond to you positively. It is important to share the script with the staff, and train everyone on how to respond to various situations, even those unpleasant calls.

After my conversation with this client, she was happy that she had come to me to discuss the situation. I didn't focus on the situation itself, or on her feelings about it, or on trying to make her feel better. I instead focused on finding the best way to move forward. Had she not contacted me or asked for help from someone, she might eventually have found a solution, but she could have spent sleepless nights thinking about it.

Part of you may wish that certain situations never happened, but in reality, the experience can teach you invaluable lessons. In the case I just shared, there are a couple of things you could do to improve the situation: contact the client, be upfront and honest, and most will appreciate it. Then, thoroughly investigate what went wrong—machine error or human error—and find out how to minimize the chances this situation or a similar one will happen in the future. Once you know the answer, it is time to take action, and set up new rules. At the end of the day, gather your team, share with them and let them share their experiences with everyone else and make sure everyone on your team understands and executes the solution. This way, the lessons learned can be used to continue building a profitable and successful business.

By now you might be more than convinced that asking for help can save you time, money, alleviate emotional distress, help you grow and be creative and help you express yourself in the best possible way. But don't forget to trust yourself!

CHAPTER 3

Who to Ask

There is a range of sources from whom you may ask for help. While you are your best resource, this chapter will review the options you have elsewhere.

Before reaching out to your contacts, consider the following groups:

1. **Mentors:** They believe in you and in your potential and they want to see you succeed. Even when you lose touch for one reason or another, they find a way to reconnect, and to be there for you.

2. **Friends and Colleagues:** There are those who are ready to help and to accept your help! Now, that's a great combination. These are friends and colleagues who you know you can count on and who know they can count on you no matter what. These are precious relationships you need to keep nurturing.

3. **Takers:** There are those who just want to take! They love your help, and since you are always so kind, they keep coming back to you, rarely asking how you are doing, and never asking if you need anything. Be aware of them, so that you can protect yourself from doing too much for them.

4. **Paid Professionals:** Business coaches, consultants, lawyers, accountants, financial advisors, PR professionals, etc.

5. **Groups and Associations:** You can start your own mastermind group or join membership associations.

6. **Your Clients:** They can provide you with the feedback you need to make key business decisions.

7. **The Universe or Your Higher Self.**

1. Mentors

Mentors believe in you even when you're not sure you believe in yourself, even when you don't know you will succeed or what you are good at. You might seek out someone you admire and ask if she will mentor you, or sometimes, some professionals you meet are so passionate about what you are doing that they volunteer their help.

If someone is genuinely kind and wants to mentor you, and you are able to establish a relationship of trust, the value of their advice will be priceless to you. A mentor will not actually do things for you, such as create a website, write a plan, etc. You would do that yourself, with their guidance, and get feedback later. Some mentors might be willing to read the content of your website or business plan, and advise you on how to improve it, but if your goal is to have someone who will take care of an aspect of your business for you, you are better off hiring a professional.

Timing is also very important when asking for help from a mentor. When, where, and how you ask can make all the difference. If you approach a speaker a few minutes prior to her presentation, and ask her to be a mentor, she might decline, just because she is focused on her speech. If, however, you wait for her to finish, offer her positive feedback, ask her for her business card and ask if you can follow up with her soon, that could make all the difference.

It might be best to establish a relationship of trust before you ask someone to mentor you. Do this by opening up and sharing your own situation, by being clear about where you are, and how the information and feedback you receive could make a difference in your life. You have a purpose, a goal, and this person can help you to achieve it.

Whether the mentorship is offered to you, or if you ask for it and receive it, it is important to establish some basic rules:

• How often can you contact your mentor?

- What's the best way to communicate? By phone, email, in person, or a combination of the three?
- How long will the meetings last?
- When will the mentorship end?
- What's the goal of this mentorship?
- And discuss anything else that you and your mentor would like to clear up before the relationship continues.

Once those rules are established, make sure to respect them. As a mentor and someone who has been mentored myself, I realize that when major changes are happening, you might want to keep in touch with your mentor more often than usual. Make sure to bring up that possibility first, before suddenly disturbing your mentor with too many phone calls and emails.

Be careful not to cross the line and ask for too much from your mentor. The person can say no, but would you risk that mentorship for a one-time project that you need to complete on a holiday weekend? I recommend that you call the mentor to ask for a referral, and to discuss the situation, but not to ask her to get it done for you, for free and immediately. Even if she does stop what she is doing to help you, it might be hard to maintain the mentorship afterward. Don't abuse it. If you feel you have no other option, suggest that you can pay for her services, and discuss how much it would cost upfront. Don't take the help without being sure that you are comfortable with the amount that the mentor is asking.

Now, it might be nice if the mentor doesn't ever ask for something in return. But it might be wise to look for opportunities to return the favor. By returning kindness, the mentor realizes that she is in a genuine relationship. So first of all, every time a mentor does something to help you out, send a handwritten thank you note. That's an essential rule if you want to keep the mentorship. You can also ask about her business; and find out her needs, hobbies, and goals in life. To build the relationship, you can refer clients to them, and help them succeed as much as they are helping you to do the same.

Make a list of the mentors in your life right now, and those who have helped you in the past. Are you in a position to help them now? What can you do? Sometimes an email with a link to an article is enough. Once I was reading a leadership article in a business magazine, and I remembered we had discussed the subject in a graduate business class a few years earlier. I sent the article to that professor, who had been a mentor. He was impressed that I remembered what he had taught in class a few years earlier, and I'm sure he was pleased to receive the article.

2. Friends and Colleagues

The second group on my list of people to ask for guidance is wonderful: Those who are ready to help and accept your help. You help others because you want them to succeed, you don't need to be asked, and you don't need to ask. There is an unwritten rule that friends support each other no matter what. This is not about keeping score.

It's nice to have a sounding board for ideas. This doesn't mean that you need to follow everything that your friend, mentor or advisor is telling you. Take the advice and use your best judgment. And it's okay if you choose not to take action on a suggestion; there is no need to explain why you are not pursuing their idea. But if asked, just say that you wrote down the idea, and that when the time is right, you will consider pursuing it.

3. Takers

Now, let's discuss the third group. When you are a giver, you give every time people contact you. Be aware of people who might want to take advantage of you, so that you save your time and energy for those who are ready to help in return, and for growing your business. At first, you may consider them to be friends, but stay aware of the fact that these relationships are one-sided. Even if you choose to ask for help from takers, be advised that they most likely will disappear and not help you. Remember not to become a taker yourself, and to give back when opportunities arise for you to do so.

4. Paid Professionals

The fourth group is composed of professionals, business coaches, consultants, lawyers, accountants, financial advisors, marketing experts, and others whom you can hire. I will discuss business coaches in more detail next.

Business Coach

Before hiring a coach, consider the type with whom you would prefer to work:

- One who tells you the truth and offers unfiltered advice (even when it's painful)
- One who says what you want to hear
- One who believes his or her ideas are the only way
- One who allows you to express your best self and helps you reach your potential
- A combination of the above

There are all kinds of professional coaches providing business assistance. I've also learned that some of them can crush your dreams. If this happens to you, ask for help somewhere else as soon as possible.

When you choose to work with a coach, it can be a good idea to work with someone whose style is different than yours. This can help you learn different ways of doing things, but it can also be nerve-wracking. One of the people I mentored approached me to say that she was so nervous about a project she was starting the following week that she couldn't sleep. She was following the lead of her manager, who was micro-managing each step of the project, and after days of working together, they had accomplished less than 10% of what needed to be done. She asked for my help, and within a couple of hours, we had prepared the skeleton of the project. I shared my method with her and told her how I felt comfortable with looking at the big picture first and then filling in the blanks. She enjoyed working together and was thankful for that approach.

If a coach's approach is not helping you, and is instead making you feel unease and stress, feel free to approach her to discuss it. On the one hand, it could mean that she is on to something that you perhaps feel is hard to accomplish. On the other hand, it could mean that you need to move faster, slower or in a different direction. My recommendation is that you don't wait until it is too late to discuss how you are feeling. Approach your coach as soon as any uneasy feelings arise. You might be resisting something great, and you could be afraid of the results, or her method might just not be working for you.

When meeting with your coach, pay attention to the old, to the new, to the obvious and to the absurd, and make sure you write down that information for future reference. This way, when some or all of the information provided by her eventually becomes relevant you will have it handy.

In a coaching relationship, making sure that the meetings are effective is up to you. Read everything in the contract, including the fine print. And be mindful that a coach is not a consultant. A consultant will actually do a lot of the work for you, study every aspect of your business and present a solution that might work for you. In contrast, a coach will address how you can conduct a thorough investigation of your business, how to prepare a strategic or marketing plan, or how to develop a management team without getting involved in actually doing it.

If you would rather have someone who is more involved, it might be better to hire a consultant. But if you hire a coach, although there will be work for you to do, you will probably learn more about business and your own venture than if you hire a consultant.

How to Find and Hire a Coach

There are many ways to find a coach. You might meet one you'd like to work with at an event, where you can ask him/her the best way to follow up. You can find coaching organizations online. Some coaches have a checklist to see if you fit their service and style, and once you fill it out and qualify, you might be eligible to receive a free coaching session by phone or in person. You could also ask for referrals from colleagues by posting a request on a social networking site.

Even if a coach is highly recommended, I suggest that before making a commitment, you take advantage of the free coaching session that might be available, and make sure that it is a good match. Usually, the first discussion about your business and needs can determine if you will be working with a person whose style you are compatible with or not. I had a bad experience once in which I was offered a free coaching session, and I felt like the coach's style and answers were being forced on me. Obviously, I did not hire that coach.

Coaches who are ready to challenge you are more valuable than those who are agreeable. You don't need to hire someone to agree with you. You can agree with yourself!

If you prefer to send the potential coach an email and you don't hear from them, don't assume that they received it and decided not to respond. I've been through many situations in which the person didn't get my message, or I didn't get hers. We could have incorrectly assumed there was a problem between us, or something was wrong, when in reality the emails sent never arrived at their intended destination or went to the spam folder. I recommend that you try reaching your coach by phone to make sure that the connection is made.

If the subject is delicate or complex issues are being discussed, the best thing is to meet face to face. Even when I'm coaching by phone and by email, I prefer to discuss certain aspects of my clients' business in person, such as one's financial projections and their marketing materials. This way, you can be sure to be looking at the same file and it is easier to bounce ideas back and forth. On the other hand, recent technological advances enable you to work with a coach online and use Skype, MSN or other messengers, and software that allow you and your coach to work on the same file at the same time.

Contract

When hiring a coach or most paid professionals, the rules will be established in the contract. The contract usually states the number of hours of coaching you get, how many in-person and phone meetings you'll have each week, and if you can exchange emails (and how many) between meetings. Some coaches offer unlimited emails, others offer emails with a limit or price attached, while others don't offer email services at all but might allow you to call for a quick update between the coaching sessions. If you feel like you need additional services, make sure to discuss them upfront. Everything you agree upon should be included in the contract.

Consultants and other business professionals might charge a fee per project, or a retainer, which means you pay a monthly fee and agree on the services that will be provided for the period of the contract. Make sure the contract states exactly what will be charged for each month and how long it's going to take to execute the project. Read the cancellation policy carefully too, and make sure it is reasonable.

It is important to find someone who has your best interest at heart and is willing to help you succeed. It is possible that you might choose to change coaches; perhaps because the coach doesn't think your idea can happen soon enough. As long as the contract allows, it is your choice to move on. However, if that coach is willing to help you get to where you want to be, by encouraging you to start from where you are today, I'd listen.

5. Groups and Associations

Mastermind Groups

The basic idea of a mastermind group is that you invite like-minded individuals who are working toward a particular goal, to meet often and support each other. Although you don't necessarily have the same goal, you come together to provide motivation and accountability as you all achieve your goals. One person acts as the moderator, and that role can rotate among the members. The moderator makes sure that everyone has some time to speak and to receive feedback from the other participants. The meetings of your mastermind group can be held over the phone or in person. If you have something you've written, or if you have a writers' group, you might be allowed to share your writing with the group in advance, so that they can come prepared to offer you feedback. Or you could just come to the meeting with your questions, and use it as a brainstorming session. You could either start a group or you could join an existing group.

To the best of your ability you can invite people you trust to join your group. I'd still recommend that you set up ground rules from the beginning. Make sure everyone understands that by participating they are agreeing to respect certain rules of confidentiality, respect, support, trust, and willingness to share their knowledge with the group. Determine upfront what constitutes unacceptable behavior, the consequences and how you are going to reinforce the rules, so that everyone understands the appropriate behavior. For example, if someone starts talking about your idea at other meetings, unless they have your permission, this might be a huge red flag. If the rules are discussed in advance, then that person won't be surprised when you ask him/her to leave the group immediately.

You could include people who you know might challenge you, although you need to be careful not to get stuck by what they say. It might be a good idea to have a combination of personalities and professions at various levels of experience, those who've been through a challenging situation that you are facing, as well as those who are just starting out, and can bring a fresh perspective to the group. Plus, once trust is established, you can ask the group difficult or more personal questions and get a straight answer. Brainstorming sessions will allow you to get different perspectives on your challenges and possibly help you to figure out solutions and simple actions you hadn't thought of before.

The meetings can involve goal setting, goal execution, or brainstorming which goals make the most sense to you and the participants at the moment. In addition to getting new ideas on the spot and staying motivated, a mastermind group can be an excellent source of peer accountability. The group will hold you accountable and ask you if you've taken the required steps that were discussed during the previous meeting. It becomes harder not to take action, and if you don't, be sure to do some self-reflection before the meeting to find out the main reason for why you did not start pursuing your goal. There are no right answers here; it might be that a lot of things were going on in your personal and professional life, and you had no other motives for avoidance. Or it might be that you didn't feel comfortable taking certain actions. If the latter is the case, you could discuss how you are feeling with the group. You may find out that you are not alone, and others are feeling the same way.

Associations

There are many associations that you can join that connect you with other entrepreneurs. When deciding which association to join, a little bit of legwork and research might be required. It might be as simple as reading about each association's target audience. Some of them only accept members whose businesses have broken the $1M or $2.5M mark, such as the Women President's Organization, while others like the National Association of Women Business Owners does not have such restrictions. There are associations that are specific to one industry, for example, Women in Communications or Women in Technology. You might want to consider an association that is specific to your own niche. Others might help you to stay up-to-date on the latest market trends and offer you assistance with the business issues you face depending on your type of business and industry. My recommendation is that before joining an association, you attend one of their meetings or events, to make sure it's a good match, and if possible, to interview one of its members.

Questions to ask an association's member:

- How long have you been a member?
- Why did you join?
- How satisfied are you with the association?
- How has it helped you and your business?
- Are you planning on renewing your membership? Why? Why not?

Even though it's important to be a part of an association that represents your industry, joining an association that assists a variety of businesses can help you get different perspectives. It can inspire you to innovate your industry by transferring methods and systems from another, and it can provide you with a network of companies and services that you can use for your own business.

If your budget for joining a networking group is nonexistent at this time, consider looking for assistance from the U.S. Small Business Administration (SBA) resource partners: Women's Business Centers (WBC) at a local not-for-profit organization— the focus of the WBC is to assist women in starting and growing businesses, or Small Business Development Centers (SBDC) at a college near you, or Counselors to America's Small Business (SCORE - Volunteer retired executives to assist with your business needs). Most of them provide low cost or free assistance to entrepreneurs, as well as networking opportunities. In New York, there are city, state and federally funded programs available to assist micro and small businesses, and there are similar programs throughout the United States. A few places to start are your own city and state websites; they will offer the information you need to locate a business center near you. Those websites will also contain information on business opportunities, steps to become certified as a woman business enterprise (if your business is at least 51% woman-owned), and for doing business with the government. Another useful resource is the U.S. Small Business Administration site, www.SBA.gov, which provides online classes and a list of all resource partners located around the country. Several centers have started to provide remote technical assistance, so that you can receive help by phone or email as well.

Business centers also have coaches at different levels with different intentions and values. Just like with any coach you might hire, if you don't feel like you connected to one coach, ask for another coach within that agency, or try another agency.

The Expert

The five groups I discussed so far give you many options when seeking help, but whom do you choose? Trusting an expert who has done what you're trying to accomplish before makes sense, doesn't it? It does when she has been through it and has succeeded in establishing a successful company, and she is willing to reveal the steps or at least share her experience. On the other hand, if you are consulting with someone who has always worked for large companies and has a success vision that is aligned to corporate America, you need to be wary of the information she shares. It is as important to discuss your idea with an expert who knows your industry as it is to discuss it with someone who understands small businesses, and knows how they are built and how real growth most often does not happen overnight.

My experience has been that if your intuition is telling you that the ideas being offered might not work with your business, you are probably right. Our tendency is to believe that since we are dealing with experts, who were highly recommended, we have no reason to question them. However, experts might have different perspectives on how to best run and grow your business. Their knowledge and theories might reflect situations they've experienced while running well-established companies, which might not be the reality of your business at the moment.

If you feel the slightest doubt about what is being said to you, take another moment to reflect on it, and perhaps discuss it with your support network (which may include a mastermind group). Go even further and analyze the positive and negative results that could occur, and which ones are most likely to happen. Once you have an idea of the big picture and the immediate consequences of that plan, you can make a wiser decision about the best course of action to take.

As discussed earlier, an idea that works for one person and business, might not work for yours. An idea that works for you might not work for someone even running a similar business. That's what makes us all distinct individuals, capable of creating businesses, with even the slightest difference that set us apart from our competitors.

When discussing your idea with an expert, make sure to add your own perspective and pursue a combination of ideas that works for you and your business. As a woman running your own business, you bring to the table unique qualities and skills that nobody else has, and it can make a difference in the long run. That uniqueness can make people choose to buy from you rather than from your competitors, independent of the dollar amount you spend in advertising and promoting your business. Furthermore, by doing something unique and outside the box, the business might generate free publicity.

6. Your Clients

Asking clients for feedback is something that many corporations do and, although simple, not many small business owners invest in it. I had clients who came to me and said, "Yellow Pages just called me, they want me to renew my ad, what do you think I should do?" The first question I ask is if they received any results from the first ad. How would you know? Simple, every time a new client contacts you, or walks into your store, you could ask, "How did you hear about us?" Or, if you are placing an ad, sending postcards, or sending out direct mailings, you could create a special code for each venue, with a promotional item. This way, you can determine which ads are performing the best, and which ones you should drop or improve. Once you collect the answers from a considerable amount of clients, you can review your marketing strategy.

You could also survey clients to find out their opinion about your products/services. Depending on the survey's complexity, it may be less costly and time-consuming to hire a professional to collect and interpret the data, or you could use one of the online survey tools, which allows you to get instant response from customers. As you receive feedback from your clients, you may get great testimonials, and you can ask your client's permission to use her comments on your website and marketing materials. To demonstrate that the testimonials are real, you should include what you did for that client, the results achieved, as well as the client's full name, city and state, and when available, a link to their website.

Before launching a new product or service, it's always good to test it in the market. Remember to have a list of informal questions to ask your clients. "What do you like about the new product? How could it be improved?" And if you are not the person on the floor, dealing directly with the clients (and as your business grows, you probably won't be), train your staff to ask strategic questions, and to write the answers and share them with you.

Most people like to talk about themselves and their experiences, so an informal conversation will be easy. For more formal questionnaires and surveys, having a prize for those who fill it out may make a difference. It could be a coupon with a discount or cash value to be used on their next purchase, or a short report, sent as a pdf file, with useful information for your clients. For example, a professional organizer might write and offer a free report: "10 Basic Tips on How to Organize your Office," as something to show appreciation for her client.

Your clients might know what they need, but just because you get one client's suggestion, does not mean that you need to make a change right away. The best thing would be to survey a number of clients and make sure that the proposed change pleases many. If a client keeps asking you to make a banana cake, and it is not on your menu, are you going to test it and create an item because one customer wants it? Not so fast. You can consider creating one for this client, and charge accordingly (a higher price than the regular cakes due to testing costs and exclusive recipe), but you don't necessarily have to launch it worldwide. You could, however, offer that product as a possibility for other clients to place special orders, and once it becomes a good seller, it might be time to consider adding the item to the regular menu.

Other than soliciting feedback from clients, you can also learn from their purchase behavior. You can observe the products or services that are not selling. Would you keep a sandwich on the menu that nobody ordered for years, and that you need to buy fresh ingredients for each day? If you have done so, it is time to change. It is time to observe your best and worst sellers and find a way to modify or remove the items that are not selling.

In addition to asking clients, you can research which products and services are more often solicited, and which ones not at all. Not keeping an inventory system yet? It's never too late to start one. A simple Excel spreadsheet can help you, or of course you could consider using more advanced bookkeeping software, such as QuickBooks.

7. The Universe/Higher Self

When thinking about asking for business help, I couldn't leave out point number 7 on my list, asking for Universe/Higher Self guidance. I have always asked for guidance, and I believe it's possible that even the answers within us might be coming from many sources. Whether you ask for specific, targeted questions and listen, or sit quietly and wait for clues on the best course of action to take, guidance from a Universal source can help in the decision-making process.

When things are not going as planned ask yourself:

- What is the lesson here?
- How can I look beyond this situation to find a solution?
- What would be a wise action to take now?

And wait for the answers to come to you. By looking beyond the facts and listening to the voice within, you will learn to realize that for every challenge there are lessons and blessings. Once you recognize the lessons, you will be able to move forward and find solutions.

During stressful business situations, when you feel like you are at the edge and about to lose your patience, hope, faith, or confidence, stop for just a moment, breathe and realize that there is more to life than that moment. Just a short, brief break to attune with the Universe and with your heart, can help you to change your perspective.

When I'm unsure of what to say during a business meeting, or if I should speak up at all, I wait for the right answers to come to me. Even when your impulse drives you to speak up, make sure it is the message you want to express. Sometimes delaying to reveal information might turn out to be the best action. If at a later time, after you have a chance to reflect, you still feel the need to share your opinion, feelings, or impression of the situation, then go ahead and do it with confidence. Asking for help from the Universe or your Higher Self is a tool that you need to constantly practice in order to master it.

Consciously I have surrendered problems a few times and have been pleasantly surprised when, in just a few hours, solutions have come to me. But we can soon forget that we can trust a force that is beyond ourselves. We try to hold on to our problem and we keep struggling to find a solution, until we are ready to tell ourselves that we've done everything we could have, and that now it is time to allow things to work out as they will.

Another method is to believe that the situation is solved from the beginning. If you want to develop this, start by paying attention to how you feel about giving over a solution to a problem, and test yourself by surrendering or giving over simple things at first. Once you see that this works, you can move on to major issues.

You might develop your own way of asking for help from the Universe. You might meditate on a question, take time to review a problem before acting on it, or breathe deeply and wait quietly for an answer to come to you. Most importantly, trust your own intuition.

Who Has the Answer?

All of us have a number of people in our lives whom we call friends or acquaintances. We may have confidants and we may have a pub pal, a movie friend, a theater buddy, a work colleague, a business partner, etc. We know exactly who to contact in certain situations, but sometimes we are so confused that we might ask more than one person to help us.

One time during one of my career transitions, I had three job offers and wasn't sure which one to pursue. One job opportunity would offer the potential to make more money but no security, one offer included security but not much money, and then there was a challenging offer with a medium salary. When asking my friends about these possibilities, I got different opinions from each person.

When you have as many opinions as options, which one do you pursue? Some people may advise you to make lists of pros and cons, others might suggest that you meditate. And I say do both, or do something completely different to take your mind off the problem, and the solution will come to you later.

Make peace with the fact that mistakes can happen, and that a decision might cost more than you anticipated. Know that you may need to take corrective actions later on. This reduces the pressure of trying to be perfect. There isn't such a thing as the perfect match, the perfect contract, or the perfect partner. What exists always is room for improvement, space to grow, and opportunities to learn. If things are not going exactly the way you imagined, don't wait until things really get out of hand before changing your strategy.

When faced with many options, investigate the possibilities, and analyze why the person advising you thinks you should pursue one option at the cost of another. It might be that they have their own fears and therefore are advising you from that point of view. Or they might have had experiences with pursuing that path and it didn't work for them. Therefore, make sure that the advice is grounded.

At this point, you actually might already have a group of mentors, you might be a part of a mastermind group, and you might be working with a coach. How do you know if any of these people has all the answers? You don't, and most likely, you will need to ask more than one person.

The decision about who to contact can be made easier if you start grouping and organizing your contacts into areas of expertise. The categories might look something like this:

- Business Expert
- Technology
- Finance
- Marketing
- Managing staff
- Industry-specific expert
- Product Development expert
- Life Coach

- Professionals in your city (Dept. of Consumer Affairs), state (licenses and permits) and federal agencies (IRS, SBA), or elected officials.
- Other professionals with whom you do business (lawyers, accountants, bankers, insurance brokers, financial advisors, etc.).

You can add as many categories as you would like. This will help you to take some time to step out of the problem, so that you can see which category is best for your needs. And you will reduce the number of calls to people who won't be able to help you. Some people on your list might be more attentive when your call is about something they can really help you with. You could also create personal goals to meet someone in each area, or to add those you are missing to a mastermind group, or a professional network.

You could also invite four to six of those professionals to form an advisory board. The group could meet with you a few times a year to discuss your business and the best strategies you could pursue. The advisory board's role is only to advise you, so that you decide the best course of action.

For advice, the best person to ask is someone you trust, but sometimes it's hard to know whom you can trust. If you are discussing proprietary information, make sure to somehow protect yourself from those not so ethical individuals who cross your path. See Chapter 4 for more information on this.

Clearly there are many sources of help available to you. How can you decide where to go to get help? First of all, research the options available, take a look at the reference chapter at the end of this book for more information on agencies and directories, and follow up with them. Second, consider your budget: Can you invest in a membership or in hiring a coach at this time? Third, before joining an association, attend a few events to make sure it is going to be advantageous for your business; and before hiring a coach, contact referrals and ask if you can attend an exploratory free first session before signing the contract. Fourth, find out if the members of the organization you are considering joining either need your products or services and can potentially become your clients or if they have something of value to offer you. If they have no interest in your products/services, and have nothing to offer to you, you may consider seeking other organizations that have the potential to deliver a professional benefit beyond advice. Fifth, when going to a non-profit or a WBC, or the SBDC, or SCORE, make sure to ask for someone with experience in your industry—it makes a huge difference. Finally, always check in with yourself and with your own intuition.

CHAPTER 4

How to Ask for Help

When you decide where to go for help, how do you ask for it? First of all, be open. Ask for help with an open mind, and trust that you are at the right place, talking to the right person, no matter what comes out of the meeting. You can come with your own questions prepared, or you can stay open, just state the issues you are facing and let the coach determine the real problems. A number of times, my clients have come to a meeting determined to discuss a certain issue, but as soon as the conversation starts I realize there are more important issues hidden beneath the surface.

I have had a chance to assist many different personality types, and different businesses in a variety of industries. Every now and then, there is the know-it-all client. At first I worked hard to come up with creative ideas they hadn't thought of, but soon realized my efforts were pointless. They knew it all already. If there's a know-it-all in you who occasionally surfaces when you are managing your business, you might be limiting your potential to learn, and you might be missing out on alternatives you haven't thought of.

When asking for help, I suggest that you do a self-inquiry on the type of person you are, and how open you are to listening to other perspectives on the issues you are facing or might soon face in your business. You might have most of the answers, and that's fine. How about the questions you did not think of asking? Being open to receiving advice will make a huge difference in your business.

Allow yourself to remain open when running your business, in order to come up with wild ideas, even if you think you would never pursue them. This will help you adjust your mindset, and allow you to become aware of the possibilities available to you. You can choose traditional paths, or you can create your own creative and new path.

How to Listen and Filter the Information

When receiving advice, it is important to understand that not all information is useful. Although you need to be open to receiving what others are saying, you also need to decide for yourself what to pursue, what to ignore, and which actions to take next.

You can't imagine how many people suggested that I transform my website into a blog when I was building my business. It was a good idea, but I just wasn't ready to pursue it. It is important to know yourself and your limits, so that you don't think you need to go bungee jumping when others tell you to do so. When it's natural for you, and you are bungee jumping like a pro, you will only laugh at how frightened you were early on. There is no need to say, "I can't believe I didn't try this five years ago," because you just weren't ready then.

Why do I recommend listening and filtering the information? Because the reality is that no one knows your business and personality better than you do. As I've mentioned, you need to do what feels right, and I'm a firm believer in following your intuition with caution. If your instincts are telling you to cross the street now, you still look right and left to make sure that there isn't a car coming.

What are the rules of listening and filtering information?

- Listen carefully
- Rephrase what has been said to confirm that you've heard and understood the information.
- Listen
- Reflect on what was said.
- Ask follow up questions.
- Listen
- Respond
- Reflect again
- Choose what's best for you, even when it seems difficult.

In the end, your decisions should always be about you and your business. It's up to you to decide your next steps. It's up to you to determine when you are ready, and at the same time, it's up to you to hold back.

It is important to know how to weigh the suggestions you receive. If you meet someone on the subway or on the street, and you don't know anything about this person, but she advises you to jump up and down three times to make your business grow, would you do it? Your first impulse might be to say "No way!" However, think again. Imagine that this person is a master at running businesses, and has built not one but many multi-million dollar companies. Yes, although the advice seems absurd, you might actually consider taking it. I know I would.

If you have a chance to meet successful people, even if they're not in your particular industry, it's a good idea to listen, even if their advice sounds absurd like the aforementioned example. When you don't understand why an idea was mentioned, you might want to ask the basis for their recommendation. How might that action change your business for the better?

The fact is that you can learn how to make an absurd idea work, or you can do nothing, or you can act on something that does not work. The key is to do the research, and create a plan that works for you and for your business.

It's best not to discard advice that you receive from others. At the very least, have an "Absurd Ideas' Notebook," because some day those ideas might make sense to you.

In addition, you can better filter information by preparing a list of follow-up questions for the person you are working with. Here are a few examples:

- How do you think this is going to work?
- What are the results I could expect? Positive and Negative?
- What's the best-case scenario? And the worst?
- How can we measure the results?
- Have you done this before? If yes, what results did you obtain? If not, could you recommend someone who has?
- How can I best prepare myself for this change/action?
- What's the plan?
- How do we execute the plan?

How do you listen to and filter the information? You do not take anything for granted. You listen to others' comments, and you reflect on them. If they are too wild for you to pursue at this moment, do not discard them completely, write them in your Absurd Ideas' notebook and go back to them in the future.

How Does the Advice Make You Feel?

When you sit with a counselor, coach, consultant or mentor, and what he or she is saying resonates with you, and makes you feel really great, there is a large probability that you will act on it. Conversely, if the comments feel threatening, and inconsiderate, you may leave the meeting feeling worse than when you arrived. And believe me, this happens frequently. Since I have coached many clients, I've seen people pleasantly surprised by my positive approach, since they were traumatized by previous experiences with other business coaches. While others might have felt disappointed by the reality check I provided.

Rules of thumb when meeting with a coach:

- Carry a notebook to every meeting, and take notes. Even if you have the best memory.
- After the meeting, highlight the notes and ideas that make the most sense to you or the ones that you are most comfortable with.
- Depending on the number of actions that was given to you, number them by priority and importance.

- Reflect on the suggestions to figure out how you feel about them.

- If you don't feel the ideas make sense to you, get someone else's opinion; make sure they make sense to someone you trust.

- Start taking a small step today to get you closer to achieving each goal.

Protecting an Idea

It is important to protect your ideas and your business. But doing so it isn't always straightforward or intuitive. If someone hears you talking about your idea and alters it to make it his or her own, there isn't much you can do about it. Of course you can copyright your work if you are an author of "original works of authorship", or you can trademark a word, phrase, symbol, design or a combination of them. If it's a new invention, once you have the prototype and project ready, you can then patent it, to further protect your intellectual property (Ask your lawyer if it would be appropriate and worthwhile to do so).

Keep in mind that sometimes, even a slight modification, like when someone puts what you wrote into his or her own words, can make it theirs. The reality is that the idea is only one part (even if the necessary first part) of the whole creation process. Once you have it, and you write it down, it still may not be worth much. The real value lies in executing and implementing the idea.

Some entrepreneurs carry around a non-disclosure agreement, and that's a valid approach, but many business professionals (coaches, consultants, potential partners, investors, etc.) will not sign one since a lot of the information in a business plan is similar to other plans. It's best to ask that the professional not use your idea, unless they have your permission to do so. You can find samples of non-disclosure agreements (NDA) online, and you can learn more about copyright, trademarks and patents by visiting the U.S. Patent and Trademark Office website at www.uspto.gov. You may—in fact, should—also consult with an intellectual property lawyer to find out the best way to protect your idea or project, bearing in mind the costs and benefits of protection.

What If Your Idea Is Stolen . . . Or Pops Up Elsewhere?

Don't spend too much time worrying about whether someone will steal your idea. Use that energy to stay motivated and to actually follow through on your project, and to take steps to move it closer to being realized.

If your idea is stolen, you have two options: (1) create something else; or (2) bring a lawsuit. Once again, you have to weigh the costs and benefits of each option for that particular situation. The advantage to the "create something else" approach is that you train your mind to be creative; you could launch a new product, a new service, or a new combo at least once a year! Remember that change is an important formula for staying in business for years to come.

On the other hand, there could be a substantial benefit to pursuing legal action if you have strong evidence of the steps you've taken to protect your idea, whether with an NDA, copyright, trademark, or patent. If you haven't taken any of these steps, it might be harder to pursue a lawsuit, but you should consult with a lawyer to find out your options. Keep in mind that pursuing a lawsuit can be very costly, emotionally draining and time consuming. And, as I mentioned, the best action might be to focus on creating a new product or service instead.

Sometimes, when you focus your attention on a project, you might begin to notice the same subject popping up around you. I experienced several examples of synchronicities that happened around most of the themes we chose for WomenandBiz.com. Moreover, when I started writing this book, I learned of other business guides for women entrepreneurs that were being published. At first I felt discouraged, but now I realize that the Universe was just saying, "Yes! Yes, you are on the right track." Understand that your idea could be supported by other projects available in the market, and know that you can always find a way to make yours unique.

Business attorney, Nina Kaufman, Esq., founder of AskTheBusinessLawyer.com, suggests "if you have an idea right now, but you are afraid to discuss it with another business person, you may want to talk to an attorney to assuage your concerns. Attorneys are bound by strict confidentiality rules. From them, you can learn what next steps you can take to provide more "meat" to your idea than can be protected. Plus, they can give you guidance on the kinds of situations where NDAs are appropriate, what the NDA should include, and whether it's reasonable to expect someone (a potential investor, perhaps) to sign it."

Getting Feedback without Exposing the Whole Concept

Fear of having an idea stolen can be a reason to make a person feel stuck, and think that they need to reinvent themselves or come up with a new idea. In some cases you might need to do so, or you might just need to give your concept a new twist. However, if you don't pay attention to the signs around you, you might not know that others have similar ideas until it's too late. Not researching your competitors and understanding the market because you believe your idea is unique (and will stay so *forever*) can be a big mistake for your business. Pay attention to your competition!

As a business coach, I've tried to help people who would say that they had an exclusive idea they were going to patent, but they wouldn't tell me what it was or what solution it was going to provide. I was able to offer them advice on the common business denominators that exist in all businesses, but I wasn't able to provide specific input or to figure out exactly what they needed. All I could do was ask them questions they could ask themselves later on, and leave them to try to figure it out on their own.

One option is, when possible, to not share the idea with your coach or consultant in full, but to only offer enough information so that you can brainstorm to get some feedback on it. Without sharing your idea, you can still share the problem you are solving and the need you identified. Here is an example: "You know when you go to the supermarket and you spend a while looking for a product? I'm inventing a solution that will cut the product search time by half!" Although I can imagine a few ideas for this invention, I probably wouldn't be able to come up with the same solution, but I can now ask follow-up questions. "Are you going to be selling it to supermarkets or to the consumer? Is it going to be a stand-alone product, or would the client need to buy additional hardware or tools? Would it work in any supermarket or would each one need different settings? Are you going to produce it yourself, or outsource the manufacturing?"

Here are some more general questions that I probably wouldn't even think of asking, if I didn't at least have an idea of what the client in this example intended to do: "How much would it cost to produce? How much is the market willing to pay for it? How would you promote it? Who would make the decision to buy it? How are you going to distribute it? According to your research, how many people would be willing to adopt it?" Some questions might not make sense depending on the actual product or service being developed, but the idea could get the conversation going.

If you've made the decision to ask for help and you're concerned about protecting your intellectual property, consult with a lawyer, ask for referrals and ask yourself:

- How can I know if I can trust this person? What questions should I ask to find out?
- What can I do to protect myself, so that this person doesn't copy or misappropriate my idea?

Before hiring a coach or consultant, I recommend that you ask for referrals. You can talk to their clients and ask the following questions:

- How long have you worked with this coach/consultant?
- What is the best recommendation you can give about this professional?
- Why should I hire/not hire this person?
- How much did you trust this person, and was it worth it?
- Would you hire her again?

Remember, the main issue is to execute your idea. Having an idea is one small step toward your ultimate goal. Instead of focusing too much energy on protecting your idea, invest in making it happen.

Being Flexible

How flexible are you in pursuing your business vision, developing your product, and creating a new service? I've found through the years that when you have a vision for your business, but it's not working out, you still want someone to help you make it happen as you envisioned it. I once had a client who had been struggling with production costs, and we discussed several solutions—one being to offer an alternative product which would cost little or nothing to produce using the internet, but that would achieve the same or similar results for the end consumer, and would allow her to charge market price. At first she said, "Could I do that? I'm not sure how that could work…" I then spent some time giving examples of other products and how it could work. She got it, or at least I thought she did.

But by the end of the meeting, she was back to her original idea, and asked, "Could I place an order and sell it below cost just to get going?" I have to stop here for a moment, and just say that the answer to this question 95% of the time is NO. You could for example give away something for free in exchange for a purchase, but then the cost of that product should include the cost of the giveaway as well. You could also give away an e-book when people sign up for your membership fee based program. In both cases your free product or discount costs are covered by a later purchase. But when you are selling just one product, and there is no upsell or future sales, you cannot sell it below cost, period.

After the meeting I realized that the idea she had and wanted to execute was her baby. She had been dreaming about it for a long time, she wanted to see it happen her way, and she did not allow herself to be flexible towards finding a new solution to the development of her product. The obstacles or the amount of money that it would cost didn't matter, what mattered to her was seeing her products on the shelves.

How about you? Do you have a vision for your business, that you believe you can only pursue it a certain way? Are you so certain about what you want that, even with all the obstacles, you are still thinking of taking these risks? If you haven't been able to come up with an effective production cost, go back to the drawing board immediately. Give yourself the flexibility and freedom to look at your options upside down and sideways. Look for other manufacturers for example, and try to accomplish your goal by keeping the end in mind. You are creating this product/service to fulfill a need. In the case of delivering a workshop, for example, could the need be fulfilled by a Webinar rather than having to reserve an expensive conference room?

With the Internet, it is possible to come up with affordable solutions without compromising the end results. One of the obstacles I often hear is, "Elisa, I can't create the designs because my budget doesn't include the particular software I need." Maybe you could find open source software online, that would allow you to achieve the same results, or you could visit the local libraries. They might have the software that you need installed on their computers, which you could use for free. There is almost always a way. What might not exist is the perfect solution at the moment, but there are certainly options and brainstorming about them can be key to your success.

How to Accept Help

There are times when you or your business reaches a crossroads. In those times, you will most likely be able eventually to find a solution to your situation, and you will move on one way or another. Nevertheless, there might be faster, easier or more unique approaches than you are aware of. Sometimes you are so focused on finding a solution one way, that you might miss an opportunity that is right in front of you. When stuck, find out what others are doing to overcome similar obstacles. Once others are helping you, accept that help with open arms and heart. You can still ponder the best ways to explore the help you are receiving, but the bottom line is that if you close yourself off, doors will close as well. Try to remain open during difficult times.

When you're offered help free-of-charge, look for ways to give back. I once was offered and accepted a scholarship to a course, without having to ask for it, which truly changed my life for the better. I said "yes" to that opportunity and made arrangements to be out of work for a few days. It was life changing. I took it graciously, and I gave my best to the course. Afterward I offered feedback to the instructors, and I believe they were happy to hear from me. I also gave them testimonials and participated in open houses for new courses they were offering. It was simple to give back to them in different ways.

If you have difficulty accepting pro-bono help, I recommend you look at it this way: By accepting help, you are providing another person with the opportunity to make a difference.

After receiving help, there are a few simple actions you can take to give back:

• Send a thank you letter.

- Stay in touch and keep the advisor informed of your progress.
- Ask if there is anything you can do, and stay open to possibilities.
- Refer clients to them.
- When your budget allows, go back for professional help that you can pay for.
- Offer a testimonial.

Receiving help starts with asking for it. Then you must follow the general rules of listening, staying open minded, filtering the information, thanking the person for helping you, taking action and giving back.

Rules of thumb to remember:

- Be polite and make sure you arrive on time and respect the other person's time.
- Be thankful—and send thank you notes.
- Be open-minded and stay alert to new opportunities.

What to Ask, What Not to Ask (If Anything)

Usually you can ask a coach any question. However, they may end up referring you to other professionals that can better help you in a specific area. When asking for advice from a coach, a mentor or others, there are a few things to keep in mind.

There is no limit to what you can ask someone, but knowing what to ask and who to ask might make a huge difference in getting an answer. The fact is that if your advisor wants to answer your question she will, but be careful not to burn any bridges with a mentor by going too far, otherwise the conversation could be over for good.

Once during one of the marketing classes I was teaching, I suggested that the participants ask other business owners about their businesses to learn more about their industry. One of the participants shared that she already visited a few storefronts in her neighborhood and asked the owners how business was doing. Most of them said it was fine. She was puzzled because she noticed less traffic in the stores and she didn't believe the owners. Well, as a business owner, you don't want to ever sound desperate to a potential client, so you'll always say that business is doing well.

There are methods you can use to get more honest responses. If you feel that the question you have in mind is difficult, you could start by approaching the subject slowly, or by giving examples of the situation and then by asking how that person would handle it. There are ways to ask a question without sounding intimidating to the other person. As much as you can, begin with an explanation before asking difficult questions, so that you don't come off as threatening. Here are a few examples:

If you are researching your specific target market and want to know how businesses in general are in your neighborhood, visit a non-competing type of business and ask to speak with the owner. Instead of having a general conversation by starting with, "How is business?" How about asking him/her this way: "Hello, I'm Joan Smith and I want to open a store a few blocks from here, could I ask you a few questions about your business and how traffic has been in the last few months?" Or you could ask: "How has the economic climate affected your business, if at all?" You are no longer a client; you are a business owner who could use the experience and knowledge of this entrepreneur to help you. Most likely, she will answer your question and perhaps tell you more valuable information that you should know. For example, she may tell you about local politics, or construction issues that can cause problems for you. Remember to send her a thank you note after the meeting, and of course, ask if she would like to be invited to your grand opening.

Before going to a meeting or approaching someone and asking a delicate question, ask yourself: Would I feel comfortable answering this question? If you wouldn't, start preparing a story to introduce the topic and then see if you would be able to answer it. If yes, before asking the question, ask yourself: Would this advisor feel comfortable with this question? If you know her well, the answer will come to you effortlessly. On the other hand, if you don't know her at all, it's worth it to spend some time preparing the reasons why you want to ask that question. Your perception about a subject might not give you exact clarity, because in reality, each person perceives a subject in their own unique way, based on their knowledge, experience, resistance and feelings toward the subject. Don't assume that if it's not a big deal to you, it's not going to be for the other person. Be honest, and ask the person if it's okay to broach a sensitive subject. Give them the option to hear the question and then decide if they'd like to answer it.

One question you should use with caution or not ask at all is: *If you were in my shoes, what would you do?* You are the only one who can make the decisions about which actions to take, so even if you feel the need to ask that question, make sure to check in with yourself first. The advisor can't ever give you an answer that would represent your own experiences. Make sure that what was said by her makes sense, and that you would feel comfortable pursuing her advice.

Check list on how to ask:

- Be flexible and patient.
- Ask for referrals.
- Protect your idea through copyrights, trademarks, patents and NDA or simply execute the idea.
- When asking for help through networking, explain the difficult questions to increase your chance of getting a response.

- Check in with yourself.

CHAPTER 5

When to Ask for Help

Knowing when to ask for help and actually taking the leap and asking, are an important step in the process of growing your business.

Do you ask for help when:

- Your business is in trouble?
- Your business is stagnant?
- Your business is growing?

How about asking for help at any stage of your business?

Let's talk about each possibility:

- Business is in trouble:

o   You are running out of money.

o   Sales have been slow for the last few months.

o   You are barely making ends meet.

Once you are struggling and you don't see a solution, you've spent all your savings and there is nowhere to turn, it is disconcerting, but it is not the end. Even if you are in this situation today, there is still hope. There are still low or no-cost marketing strategies, which could perhaps help you increase the cash flow as you raise money to invest in more expensive strategies or in research and development for a new product or service. In general, this is a terrible time to apply for a loan or borrow money, but not impossible. Usually, your personal credit might not be as good at this point. You might be thinking, "If only I had asked for help before things got out of hand, there might have been an easier way out."

Although your business and dream might be in jeopardy, you must ask for help. There is free or low-cost help you can get. But don't wait another minute. In the resources chapter, you will find a list of organizations you can contact to start changing your business and life today. You could get loans from alternative sources, such as micro-lenders, which usually lend lower amounts at a higher interest rate than a bank, but this option is still better than paying high credit card interest rates or going to a loan shark. Or you could borrow against credit card sales, or apply for a peer-to-peer lending program, or consider asking friends and family. You could also consider finding a partner. (Chapter 9 explains capital sources in detail.) Lastly, you might plan an exit strategy, in order to invest in a new project. You can sell the business or close the doors and minimize the losses. A coach or consultant can help you with these exit strategies.

- Business is stagnant:

    o You have grown to the business's maximum potential.
    o Sales are stable but not increasing.
    o You are only adding a few clients a year or just maintaining existing ones.

It is fine to want to stay stagnant but this might be a good time to go back to the exercises of self-inquiry you did in the beginning of this book, and remind yourself of your goals for your lifestyle and business success.

Even if you're comfortable that the business isn't growing, it might still make sense to get counseling to keep the business afloat, to understand the market and to be ready for any changes. There is a risk in being complacent; the competition might steal your market share and your comfortable business could be gone before you know it. Brainstorming with a business coach or mastermind group could help you analyze the market and your options for growth.

- Business is growing:

    o Sales are coming in without much effort.
    o There is no down time.
    o All projects are working.

Congratulations! You are in the best situation possible. Why ask for help now? To make sure you are able to sustain the growth. To make sure you have systems in place to support the sales, and fulfill all orders. Seeking professional input at this point will help you to come up with plans of action to keep growing, to maintain or grow the current level of sales, to consider going global, franchising, licensing, or to come up with creative ideas to increase business beyond the plateau it might reach at some point. When you are in this situation, you might choose to hire a consultant, a business coach, and/or join membership organizations that offer support to thriving businesses. You might also want to change your role, to delegate and change/improve your lifestyle by giving yourself more free time.

The fact is that no matter the stage of your business, asking for help can always benefit you and your business. How long you wait to ask someone for help is your decision. Do I think you can figure out the answer on your own? Usually yes. Do I think it's going to be as fast as if you asked the right person? Probably not. I had a client who took a business training course I was teaching, who said that if she had known when she started her business 14 years earlier what she learned in the course, her business would have been in a different place today.

Even with help, it might take a while to implement the suggestions and make the changes you are planning. In my case, I worked with a coach for a while, and he recommended a few things I was able to implement five months later. It's not that I needed more convincing, or that I needed to think about it, or ask someone else's opinion. I was certain that making these changes was the right decision, but it meant leaving my comfort zone, and therefore, I took my time to take that leap. I knew that these changes could make my business better, but I could never be 100 percent certain until I tried. Once I made the change, I was so glad I did. The transition wasn't as smooth as I would have liked, but I did it anyway. After a while, it worked out and the changes have paid off many times over.

Regardless of your business situation today, consider the opportunities that asking for help can create in your life and business. I recommend that you visit the resources listed at the end of the book to find an agency or coach who can help you, or an association that you can join, or take some time to connect with friends and family and ask for their help.

CHAPTER 6

What do you do when you don't get support?

"Your Idea Won't Happen"

Unfortunately, some coaches just say point-blank that your vision is not going to happen. You might hear, "Let's discuss your skills and abilities. Maybe there is another business more suitable to you." I suggest that you stay open to everything that comes out of this meeting, listen to why he/she believes it isn't going to work for you, and write everything down. Remember to listen and filter the information. But DO NOT under any circumstance BELIEVE that this is the truth and the only truth. If what she is saying makes sense, what can be done to change it, to overcome the obstacles mentioned? There are lessons in every meeting. In fact, you might even learn more from those who are skeptical of your ideas. They know so much about what could go wrong, that this will help you to plan for it to go right.

Many times I've met with people who have said, "I'm coming up with this new idea because when I went to see a coach, with my real twenty-year-old passion, I was told that it isn't going to happen." Why give one person, one coach, one counselor, one friend all this power?

The naysayers might not see the big picture. By wanting to help you avoid failure, they tell you that it can't be done, or that there are other ways to pursue your goal without reinventing the wheel. Don't get discouraged. Accept their opinions, go back to the drawing board, or continue doing your research. It's hard to say that every idea will become successful. But for sure, the entrepreneurs who did due diligence and homework, took their time to understand the market, to create a marketing strategy, and to develop and follow a plan of action, were able to achieve success faster than those who didn't. Of course there are entrepreneurs who decided to build their business organically, and became successful. That can work as long as you understand that it might take a while until you get a feel for the market, and until you get it right. But it can also be costly! It's better to plan ahead.

I'm not saying that it's going to be easy, and I'm not saying that your plan will develop exactly as you envisioned it. There are many issues that can get in the way of your plans, such as: the economy, politics, legal issues, your financial situation, difficulties in getting investors, the market, personal issues that need your attention, and many other challenges. Nevertheless, there is always a way to stay close to your dream. You can create a support team to help you reach it, and you can get help in creating step-by-step strategies to overcome mental, physical, emotional, and external obstacles. Stay open to all possibilities and your vision will happen.

Even when you are sitting across from a naysayer, who says that starting this business was a mistake or that you can forget about your growth plan and idea—stay alert. I'm convinced that establishing your dream multi-national company isn't impossible, as all of the existing ones today started with just an idea and grew. But you've got to build from where you are today, with a focus on where you want to go.

"Your Business Concept Does Not Work, Change it To…"

I have met with several clients who were ready to change the focus of their businesses, because they discussed their ideas with someone else who said they couldn't get clients if they were to follow their original plan. I disagreed. We then discussed if the new focus would really represent what they were proposing to do, and most of the time, it would not. I also suggested that they research their topic further. It is possible that each advisor originally advising those clients wanted them to do what was familiar and safe for the advisor, but it did not mean that it was the best option for the clients.

Ultimately, the action you choose to take is your decision, and it's best to ask yourself a few questions:

- How do the coach's ideas/comments reflect my vision for this business?
- What's the best course of action at this moment?
- Who else could I reach out to?

- Where can I further research this topic? Are there associations, trade publications, chambers of commerce I could contact?
- What's true to my business and myself?

When you feel your ideas are challenged, take a break and meditate until it is clear which option to follow. In reality, the only way to pursue an idea someone else thought of is to make it your own. For me, I need to agree with them, I need to see it happening, I need to believe in it, and most of all I need to be excited and confident that the idea can work. It is fine to follow someone else's suggestion, as long as you make it your own. Dedicate yourself to finding a solution that you can pursue, rather than committing to another person's idea without truly knowing what you are doing.

If you are convinced that the idea being offered to you works, it is time to figure out how you can make it work. What skills do you already have to develop the idea/strategy? Can you do it on your own or do you need to hire a professional? Are there skills you can learn or need to learn? Do you have any experience with a similar situation, and would it help you develop this one? You can start putting a list of your accomplishments together, and seeing how those accomplishments apply to this new strategy.

What to Do When You Hear Conflicting Messages?

When you receive two conflicting opinions about a project, what do you do? Which one do you follow? Through the years, I have come to realize that there could even be a third option. There is often another way to reach your goal; you just have to be creative.

In reality there are many ways to grow your business. You might meet a coach who is conservative, and advises you to take it slow. She might advise you to use your own funds, and grow your business brick by brick. Another advisor might suggest that you should act as if you were already a billion dollar company, and ask for a $500,000 loan or to seek investors. The third coach might be somewhere in the middle, or fall closer to the more conservative one or to the more aggressive one.

Or there might be a conceptual difference between coaches. One might advise you to diversify your line, while the next advises you to keep the line, but offer different packaging, create a unique promotional strategy, target a different niche, etc. If you are caught in such a situation, what do you do? Go back to the basics. It's going to take some work, but it's better to know what you are getting into or at least to take calculated risks.

- Start studying the possibilities suggested to you and analyzing where you are today:
    o Financially: Is your business comfortable or struggling? To what degree?
    o Management Team and Personnel: Could your current staff handle growth? Do you foresee hiring employees or professionals to help with this project? Are new employees in your budget?
    o Marketing: Have you exhausted all marketing options to promote the products/services you are currently offering? Is there a market for the proposed growth?

○ Operations: Are your current production location, equipment and machinery, and storage space able to handle more orders? If not, how much would it cost to move or to purchase additional equipment?

○ Industry Trends: How is the market at this moment? How is the competition in the area you want to grow into? Is there room for growth?

- For all the items above, start working on the investment needed, and on what's reasonable.
- Research whether you need to educate your customers in order to sell the new service/product.

For every question aforementioned, try to be as realistic as possible, and look at what you've accomplished so far. Study if the changes are aligned with your mission and vision. Again, why you started your business, and whether you ever want to sell it might come into play here, and the answers to those questions could be a determining factor.

When considering conflicting advice, ask yourself the following questions:

- Which step resonates best with me?
- Which action would I feel more comfortable with?
- What would make me feel challenged and energized?
- Which idea am I having a problem with or resisting? Sometimes resistance is a sign that that's the option to pursue. I recommend that you meditate on it, and find out why you are resisting this idea.
- How knowledgeable is my advisor? Has she applied this strategy herself, or does she have a track record of helping others in similar situations?

"I Can't Help You"

You gather the courage to ask for help, you refine your questions and you go after the person you thought would be the best match for helping you. And then the person refuses to help you for some particular reason, or for no reason at all. Do you need to stop to analyze why, and wonder what's going on? Why did this person say no? Sometimes the "no" might come because you are really supposed to ask someone else, and the original person isn't ready to be of help anyway. Just start looking for someone else, someone who is going to be a better fit than the first person. As long as you focus your energy on the person who didn't help you, you won't move on. Nowadays, with social networking growing so fast, it is easier to get recommendations quickly. Sites such as LinkedIn, Facebook, Twitter, Ryze, and many online groups, will allow you to post a question and quickly receive referrals and the help you need.

You don't ever want to burn bridges, especially when people are volunteering their time as mentors, so make sure to respect their time. If things have changed for your mentor, and you don't know what's going on in their personal or professional life, you need to give them space to say yes or no to you. If the answer is "yes", check in once in a while to make sure it's still okay for you to pick their brains. If the answer is "no", ask for another referral. Even make sure you can keep the door open, and find out if you could call again in the future. A good answer to a "no" after they helped you in the past might be to just say, "Listen, I understand you can't help me at this time, but I'll never forget what you've done for me. Would it be fine with you if I sent you an invitation to my next grand opening or when I launch the service you helped me develop?"

The way you end the conversation and handle the "no" may actually cause them to make space for you pretty soon. They set the boundaries and you accepted and respected them. In the future, when they become available, they might check in with you to see if there is anyway they can help you.

How you handle the naysayers is as important as asking for help. If you've been stuck for a while, due to what one person told you a while ago, take some time to investigate if what was said has merit. Also make sure to brainstorm with others to discuss the best possible course of action.

Remember that people around you have their own perspectives and fears, and that influences their advice to you. Therefore, check in with yourself, step back and make an effort to understand the advisor's point of view.

CHAPTER 7

Self-Awareness

When growing your business, it is key to understand and be aware of your thought patterns. You may at times feel self-doubt and start asking yourself: "Why didn't I ask for help early on?" "Why did I start this business? What am I doing? Why don't I find a full time job and forget about it?" Even though deep inside you know that none of those statements have merit. It is important to recognize that those questions are not coming from you, but from your inner-critic. There is no point in arguing with your inner-critic since you can't win. Once you acknowledge this, your self-doubt will start to lose its power over you.

There is nothing wrong with finding a full-time job or a part-time job to help pay the bills while you build your business, or to save money to invest in the business, improve your credit or gain experience. Before looking for a job, consider all available options and ask yourself if this action is in alignment with your ultimate goal. Depending on your personality, your self-doubt might be strong or not. Be aware of it, and let it go by focusing on your goal and pursuing it.

Consciousness Shifts

A lot of what happens in your business is created by your own thoughts and beliefs. I've read more books than I can count, and probably listened to as many podcasts on the subjects of Universal Laws, such as the Law of Attraction, and creating the life you want. These Laws work. As many authors and spiritual teachers will share, if you are looking to avoid certain situations, you end up receiving those same situations in many ways, so that you can avoid them.

The Law of Attraction is a very simple concept, but hard to practice, unless you make a conscious effort to stay awake and present, and observe your thoughts. The resources chapter offers a list of books that can help you shift your thoughts to help you move toward your positive goals. A student, in one of my long-term entrepreneurship classes, made the following statement: "I know that the first year of my business will be a struggle." How did she come up with that idea? And what do you think happened? She told me that her perception was common knowledge. She believed what she heard as if it were indisputable. Maybe she would be able to shift her thoughts for the second year of her business, since in her mind, it would be okay to do well at that point. I tried to shift her consciousness as soon as I heard her say that, but it was too late, her mind was made up.

But why would it be a struggle? If you're prepared, you've done your research, you know there is a need for your product or service, you have a plan and you execute the plan, why would it still fail or why would you have to struggle? It doesn't make a lot of sense. The client I just mentioned had a plan and had done all the necessary research, which was great. She was ready. But she received confirmation of the struggles by having problems with obtaining a license, and having to face other unforeseen events. Rather than spend time focusing on the negative, spend time visualizing the positive results you want to accomplish.

One of my clients is good at calling me when she needs help, but sometimes she waits too long and by the time she calls, she is already desperate. She allows the negative thought patterns to evolve to the point that she can no longer function, and then she picks up the phone. And just by listening to herself telling me the story, she awakens to her destructive behavior and before long she calls me back to say that the sale she had been working on just materialized, or that a new client came on board.

As you begin to practice being awake and present, understanding and allowing your feelings of self-doubt or others that might come up, you will be able to start changing your thought patterns and move on without being stuck for long.

Supporting Yourself

I came to realize that above and beyond the importance and advantages of the support that others can give you, is the support you can provide to yourself. If you give other people the power or responsibility to be there for you, to solve your problems, to support you no matter what, you will most certainly be disappointed at some point.

In order to avoid being dependent on others to feel good about yourself and about your business, you need to practice checking in with yourself. Ask yourself: "Why am I feeling this way? Why did that person's comments cause me to feel sad, angry, outraged or upset? How can I be present now for myself? What do I really need right now?" Once revealing answers come to you, then that's what you need to do. You are there for yourself. Sometimes this means taking a walk, taking an afternoon off, spending quality time with your family, going to the movies, eating chocolate, or playing with your pets. Other times, just acknowledging that you are there for yourself is enough, and things don't seem as huge as they were just a few minutes earlier.

Another good thing to do for yourself is to have hobbies that are important to you, and make time at least once a week to take a break and do them. You can then come back to your business refreshed and energized to keep going. For example, if you enjoy drawing, you could take drawing classes or you could buy the tools you need and start drawing and painting on your own when you have a moment to spare. If you love dancing, you can sign up for dance classes in your neighborhood, or go out and dance with friends every once in a while, or you could buy a DVD that teaches dance steps and practice them. You could go to an amusement park, you could make sure to play the instruments you love, listen to your favorite songs, walk, travel, spend time at the beach, go on new adventures, hike, read a book you never thought you would, take a class, go back to school, take a break from school, live abroad, go back home, take an afternoon off just to be with yourself, spend time with your children, and the list goes on and on. The point is that nobody can do any of those things for you. Furthermore, there is no short cut, or magic pill, you are unique and only you can experience what you need to move ahead and grow personally, professionally and spiritually.

If you feel like it, take a moment to ask yourself: "What do I need right now?" It might be that you want to continue reading the book, or it might be that you want to take a nap or that you want to go out and get things done. Just ask yourself and see what comes up. In the beginning, some people realize that they don't really know what they need, because they've been trained or trained themselves to put other people's needs first. Well, I suggest that you make an effort to put your needs first. Be with yourself and wait for something to come up. If nothing does, just consider something you used to love doing, and haven't done in a while, and see if that practice makes you feel better.

Maybe all you need is an afternoon to go to the movies and become refreshed. Then you'll have the energy and focus to dedicate 100% of yourself to your business when you return.

Resistance

Being aware of your feelings toward a coach, consultant or advisor is as important as supporting yourself through the self-awareness process. Did you ever dread going to a consultation or a meeting with your coach? Were you looking at your watch hoping that the hour would end, even though you paid for the session and chose to be there? The next time you experience this feeling, after the meeting, take time to ask yourself what was bothering you, or what you were resisting. It might be that you are not ready to make the changes being suggested.

The fact is that although it's great to have someone to hold you accountable for achieving your goals, when weeks pass by and you haven't made any changes yet, or you have taken two steps forward and three steps back, it can become stressful. If that is what is happening to you, before scheduling your next session, ask yourself a few questions:

- What am I resisting?
- Why haven't I taken the suggested action?
- What's stopping me from moving forward?
- Could I take one step today to get started? What step would it be?

Find a quiet place and time to continue with your self-inquiry, and interestingly enough, you might be resisting the answers to those questions as well. A few follow-up questions might be:

- What's the worse case scenario if I ask for help?
- What am I concerned about?
- What has been the pay off for remaining stuck?
- Why would I take this action instead of that one? Or no action at all?

- What's the source of my resistance? Is it fear? Is it my affinity for the status quo?

Once you determine the reasons why you are resisting taking action, you can be up front about it to yourself and others. If you realize that you need more information, that's what you'll bring to the table next time. If you are stuck because you are happy where you are, then is there anything else a coach can help you with? If there isn't, there is no reason to schedule another session. On the other hand, repetition pays off. If you are really committed and you agree that the advice offered is the best course of action, you can work with the counselor to help you peel away your resistance and move forward.

As I mentioned earlier, the Law of Attraction discusses the theory that what you focus on will continue to persist until you let go. If you are focusing on the lack of business your venture is going through, the lack will continue. If you focus on the prosperity and the success your business is having, you will feel better about your business, will have more energy and creatively will be able to increase sales. As you become more aligned with this concept, and you believe in your core that this law is real and possible, you will start manifesting what you want for your business. The steps to take are a combination of changing your mindset, asking questions, having a plan, accepting the guidance you are receiving, and most of all taking action toward your goals.

Here is an example of how the steps work: I could focus for hours each day on becoming a best selling author, but if I didn't write, publish and promote the book, it would be impossible to accomplish that goal. As I write every day, I also visualize the success of the book. I'm not just focusing my energy on selling books, but on how it can change the readers' lives for the better, so that they (you) can also accomplish abundance, prosperity, peace, balance, purpose and create positive change through their (your) life and business.

Checklist for self-awareness:

- Pay attention to your own behavior patterns.
- Meditate and stay alert to see beyond the challenges.
- Be present and respond to your needs every step of the way.
- Understand when and why you resist change.
- Ask for what you need.

- Trust yourself.
- Be there for yourself.
- Take action.

CHAPTER 8

Delegate

What part of your business makes you happy? Many entrepreneurs I've met built their business around their passion. Their passion to design clothing, to write, to coach, to exercise, to practice and teach yoga, to cook, to help the environment, to be around children and so much more. Nevertheless, in order to grow your business, your passion sometimes fades into the background. As the business owner, you have to take care of the daily business issues, such as bills, sales, marketing, management, personnel, operations and cash flow. Is this happening to you? Do you find yourself frustrated because of it? If not, that's wonderful. Keep doing what you are doing. If you feel overwhelmed, it might be time to start delegating some of the tasks.

Take some time to stop and calculate the value of your time. At the beginning of the week pay attention to your schedule and activities. Every day of the week write down how long you spend doing each task and calculate your hourly rate. If you calculate that your hourly rate is for example $100, and you could pay a bookkeeper $20/hour to do your books, wouldn't that be a good investment? Of course, you still need to oversee their work, but you would have more time to focus your energy on other aspects of your business. List all the tasks you perform, and see which ones you are the most productive at, and start delegating tasks that you don't enjoy as much, and tasks that you can hire professionals for less than what you pay yourself. Always make sure to check your budget first! As you build your team, remember to create a procedures manual, so that if turnover occurs, it is easier to train the new staff.

There are many options for finding help. You could start by hiring an affordable virtual assistant to help you sort your emails, pay bills, follow-up with clients, start cold calling, proofread your work, take messages, update your website, plan events, schedule appointments and so much more, possibly for a lower fee than a full time assistant. In addition, there are websites such as elance.com and guru.com, which allow you to post a task that professionals will bid on.

A business coach I worked with suggested that it was time to change my website. He suggested that I could do it myself or I could delegate the task. I was concerned about the costs of outsourcing the work, but when he told me about elance.com, I was excited about hiring someone affordable. At first I tried to figure out how to make the website changes myself, but soon realized that it would be time-consuming, time which I did not have to spare. I finally allowed myself to get the help I needed. I posted the job and hired a company in California to do it. By changing my business model, I realized that I could save time and make more money.

It felt great to have someone do the tedious work of setting up a website layout, and to copy and paste almost 200 articles from my old HTML site. It was a little scary at first, as I couldn't be sure of how well the work was going to be done, but by the end I realized that it was worth it. Prior to this change, I spent countless hours preparing the articles in the right format and posting them myself. With professional help, a new and simple system was created. Now, a website that usually would take me three full days to update takes only a few hours, and the new system is working very well.

If your business has grown to its full capacity, you can consider hiring additional full-time and part-time staff members to help you with certain tasks—tasks you haven't mastered or choose not to master, or to support you in creating a completely new product line. Remember to still keep an eye on what your employees are doing, and understand what they do, so that you can oversee their work and verify that it is done properly.

Hiring Employees

The first time I had to interview a candidate for a job was while working at my family's business. I hadn't had any training, and it wasn't easy. We decided to hire an agency to pre-screen candidates, so I asked them how one conducts an interview. They offered me basic advice and I did some research on my own. Only years later did I learn about being biased and bringing your own perceptions about a candidate to the interview, and how it can negatively affect the decision making process. When hiring, you can always ask someone else on your team to participate in the interview, so that you have a second opinion and can compare notes. Another person can help you to set your biases aside, or keep them to a minimum.

I recommend preparing a detailed job description and a list of what you want in a candidate, and then a list of questions you are going to ask him or her. If this is your first time conducting an interview, it might be a good idea to have an employment agency pre-screen candidates, and to get their advice for questions you should ask and traits you should be looking for. Remember to also find out about the legal restrictions of questions you can and cannot ask when interviewing someone. The employment agency might help you with this or you could get that information from your State's Department of Labor.

During the interview, feel free to ask the tough questions, but know their purpose and what you are looking for in an answer. Some questions you could ask include:

- What are your weaknesses?
- What do you consider your major strength?
- Why did you leave your previous job?
- Why should I hire you?

- Why are you right for this job?

In my case, practice allowed me to improve through the years. I learned a lot after hiring employees who weren't a good match. It is important to act sooner rather than later, once you figure out that a candidate is not the best option. Keeping someone longer than necessary only brings the whole energy of the team down, and once you make the decision to let that person go and you do it, things will likely change for the better. You could also consider hiring temps, and give yourself the opportunity to learn more about that employee before committing to hiring him/her long term.

If you are not willing to hire an agency at this point, consider approaching a mentor or coach, or someone in your field who perhaps has more experience than you do, and ask them the best way to hire someone, the best way to attract candidates to a position, and the best way to select them.

Alternatively, you could simply post the position on your website and send email blasts to your colleagues asking them to spread the word. Make sure to write a well-defined job description, including job requirements, skill sets and qualifications. Still, take in consideration those who don't have all the skills, but perform well in the interview, since they could eventually learn the missing skills.

Here is an example to illustrate a recruiting challenge: A client shared her distress that she let go two people who were not producing, and now she was left with a few overworked employees. A week later I asked if she had hired anyone, and she said no. I asked how she was recruiting. Did she place an ad? Did she contact a recruitment agency? Did she write a job description and send it to colleagues in the industry? Did she post a sign? No, not yet to all of them. Waiting for a candidate to knock on your door might be one approach, but is it effective? Even if or especially when you are feeling overwhelmed, it is important to take the time to announce that you are hiring. If you don't put the word out, it's going to be hard for someone to show up at your door. If they do, they might be desperate and additional due diligence might be required. Make sure always to call references before hiring someone. Through reference checks, I've always found out interesting things about a candidate that might or might not have caused the person to be hired. Either way, checking references helps you to make a better decision.

Surrendering/Delegating

Sometimes we want to control everything so much that we lose perspective of our ultimate goal. It's important to be flexible and to allow yourself to change your strategy/approach.

Once you let go of your need to control every step of your business, you will realize that situations get solved even sooner. Feel free to surrender to what's happening and allow yourself to ask for help or to give the problem over to someone else to handle. By giving up control you open yourself to finding solutions that you hadn't thought of before. When you allow a staff person to get a task done their own way, you might be surprised by his or her alternative approach. If you are constantly controlling the execution of the process instead of just overseeing the staff person's work, you might be wasting precious time and energy. Each member of your staff brings their own style, skill set, experiences and personalities and by allowing them to achieve the desired results in different ways, you can create new opportunities for your business.

Sometimes when it seems like things are getting out of control, what you need to do is relax and trust that it will work out. Too much control and not enough delegating, can keep you from learning invaluable lessons. When planning a new project, make sure you prepare in advance and ask your employees for feedback as well. Beforehand, prepare the questions you will need to ask to make sure all tasks will be accomplished. Prepare a timeline to accomplish the tasks, meet with your staff, delegate, discuss each task and make sure people are on the same page. When you are talking to an employee about an important project, make sure to give him or her your undivided attention, otherwise simple misunderstandings are certain to occur.

When delegating, simple questions to ask your staff once you've explained the task include:

- Have you done this before?
- How do you expect to accomplish this task? By when?

- What do you need to do to get it done by this date and time? Do you have all the tools you need to get it done? Would we need to purchase additional equipment, inventory, technology software or hardware?
- What are your staff requirements?
- Could you provide daily/weekly/bi-weekly reports on your progress? (Depending on the project time period, you can adjust the reporting time. If you ask for reports, make sure to read all of them!)
- What obstacles do you anticipate might make accomplishing this task a challenge?

It is best to discuss all the questions early to minimize problems and delays that might occur during the execution process.

Communicating With Your Staff

If you are not sure you understood what an employee said, ask follow-up questions. Be sure to clarify any unclear subjects so that problems don't get out of hand. One approach is to repeat what was said in your own words to confirm what you believe was said. I prefer to get to the bottom of things, instead of leaving the situation to chance, or being stuck because I didn't grasp the whole issue.

What is the most important thing to accomplish during a staff discussion? Before calling a group meeting, reflect on your goals and expectations. If you need outside input, ask for advice from your advisory board, or mastermind group. Once you have a narrower idea of the goals you would like to achieve from this meeting, it is going to be easier to communicate your vision. It is important to stay open to new possibilities, but communicate the goal of the staff meeting up front, and don't let the meeting go off on a tangent for too long or nothing will be accomplished. Make sure to bring the attention back to the agenda for the meeting. You could distribute the agenda beforehand, so that everyone understands the reasons for that meeting and has time to prepare.

How you communicate your needs in the meeting is equally important. With several employees in the room, you have at least the same number of unique opinions and getting everyone on the same page can be hard. Be sure to state the problem/issue clearly and focus the discussion toward possible short or long-term solutions. Once you've been able to clearly articulate your goal, it is time to allow the staff to brainstorm solutions. Remember to release control and allow the group to be creative. As long as you know how you feel about the subject, and are open to discussing a solution, you will be better able to welcome new ideas and receive feedback that might or might not coincide with your original plan.

Rules of thumb for delegating:

- Write a job description and know what you need.
- Post the position and get help with interviewing if you haven't done it before.
- Ask for referrals and call references.
- Train the new employees and write a procedures manual.
- Communicate what you need.
- Oversee your employee's work.
- Delegate and let go.

CHAPTER 9

Getting Help in Specific Areas

There are certain areas of your business that you might want to master yourself, while other areas you might need to delegate, or hire a professional. In this chapter, I'll discuss asking for help when writing a business plan, developing a marketing strategy and advertising campaign, and seeking financing to grow your business.

Business Plan

Regardless of how long you've been in business, having an up-to-date business plan is crucial to your success. If you wrote a plan when you first started your business, and haven't looked at it since, it is time to review it, update it, add to it, and make revisions according to the current market. If you never wrote one, it is time to do so. A sound business plan will assist you in developing a strategic plan with short and long term goals for your business, steps to achieve the goals, and it might open your mind to new possibilities. In addition, if you are considering raising funds, the business plan will be essential in the process of securing financing.

Although it takes a lot of work, time and energy to do it yourself, I recommend that you do not outsource the task of writing the business plan. There are many companies that can do it for you, and the price range varies a lot. However, they just don't know your vision or business as well as you do. I once had a client who came in with a 50-page business plan with tables, graphics, broad demographics, and some things that didn't mean much. As he was sharing his idea, I was reading his business plan, and I quickly realized that his vision for the business was not reflected in the business plan. None of it. Actually the business plan didn't clarify what he wanted to do at all. It was disappointing but we had to start reviewing and modifying the plan. He had paid a lot for a company to do it, and they weren't willing to make the necessary changes or to refund his money. Another client who was interested in opening a hair salon came in with a business plan she purchased from another company. When I asked her about it and about her promotion, marketing strategies, sales projections, unique selling proposition and licenses, she was puzzled and didn't know the answers. At that point I wasn't sure if she had read the plan. When you are not familiar with business plans, receiving a colorful and fancy one, written by a professional company might seem wonderful, but if you don't understand what's in it and your passion is not reflected in the plan, it won't help you achieve your goals.

When you write the plan yourself, not only will your passion come through the pages, but you will also learn a lot more about your business while doing the research that it entails. I recommend that you work with a coach who will give you direction and offer you a basic template to start with. Make sure to adapt the template to your needs, to create new headings and sub-headings, so that it fits your vision for the business. You don't need to make your idea fit in the original outline—you have the freedom to customize it to fit your own business. The business plan consists of at least an executive summary, business description, history and mission, business short and long-term goals, description of products and services, marketing strategy, industry trends and competitive landscape, management team, operations, financial requirements and projections with attached worksheets, and some include an exit strategy as well. Keep in mind that as the business grows and the market changes, you will need to revise and adapt the plan.

Marketing and Advertising

I've met many business owners, who either in the name of saving money, or because they wanted to express their creativity, have created marketing strategies and developed marketing materials themselves. I've done the same thing myself. Although it might be cost effective and you might receive instant gratification from those who know you did it, it just might not be professional enough.

It makes a real difference when a professional designer creates your ads, or when a marketing consultant develops a strategy for you and helps you create an effective brand. As a small business owner I've noticed that one issue is that the owner believes she is the only one who can understand the business mission and values of her business. But, if you share your vision with the marketing person or graphic designer, they might be able to capture what you are trying to illustrate better than you ever could envision.

One of the many times I created a billboard ad for my family's business, it was later criticized by one of our clients. She asked who created the ad she had just seen because it was so ugly. I hesitated but had to tell her I did it. I then followed up with a PR professional to ask his opinion about it. He didn't say that the ad was ugly or beautiful, but he said that the goal was achieved, since she still remembered the ad, and actually came to the store to share her "humble" opinion. I don't know about you, but I would rather have a client come to my business because he or she liked the ad, and it made her feel good about the company and product or service.

There are so many issues involved in producing an ad: the color, the phrases you use, the way the ads are displayed, the offer, and the list goes on. These are all factors in developing a promotion that sells. The other important point is the fact that a well-designed ad will likely generate more sales than an ad you create yourself, since a professional understands how to communicate ideas effectively. First and foremost make sure to review your budget, and find out how much money you can allocate for marketing and advertising. Major companies might spend from 10% to 15% of their budget on marketing, but whether you want to spend 1% or 30%, make sure you have the money available.

Next, decide what your goal is for the marketing strategy. Is your goal to:

- Increase sales?
- Create awareness about a new product or service?
- Promote a sale?
- Attract potential clients to the store?
- Get rid of last year's collection?

Once you know the primary goal of your campaign, it's time to quantify it. There are ways to measure the return on investment (ROI). You can keep track of your own advertising results, and use them to plan for future advertising strategies and estimate a desired ROI. If you are creating a direct marketing campaign for example, you can test the market first, by sending different sales letters to different test groups. You can then send the most successful letter to your complete list, to increase your chances of success.

Wouldn't it be wonderful if you spent $100 in a local newspaper ad and it generated 10 times more in profits? How would you know? Again, ask your customers how they heard about you. This way you can know if the ad was worth it. When you run several simultaneous ad campaigns, you can also add a unique code to each ad, which will help you identify where the clients are coming from. How do you know how much in sales you can achieve? Ask for the newspaper/magazine/TV/radio media kit; find out their audience, and what percentage of their audience corresponds to your own. Don't buy an ad just because you can afford one and you haven't advertised in a while. Do your research, contact advertisers and ask what their ROI is. The best thing to do is to call someone who is a non-competitor, and who would gladly give you the information.

I'm sure you can come up with a marketing strategy yourself, and you can also do your own PR, but it might not be as effective as if you hire someone to do it for you. On the other hand, if you are in no position to hire a professional at this time,

I recommend that you get your mastermind group together, or start a focus group, to brainstorm how to effectively promote your business, and develop a brand that speaks to your clients.

When hiring a marketing consultant or graphic designer, the same general asking-for-help-rules apply:

- Get referrals and look at the marketing materials they've created
- Ask about tangible results they've achieved
- Listen and filter the information
- Make sure to share as much about your vision for the campaign as possible
- Stay open to new and refreshing ideas

Even though I'm recommending that you stay open to new ideas, stay true to yourself, to your business mission and values, and make sure that they are aligned with the marketing campaign that is being created. In addition, read the contract to make sure you understand the number of times you can review the ad before final approval; that cost must also be included in your budget, because, more often than not, edits will be needed.

Creating an Ad Campaign

When thinking about an ad campaign, consider having a focus group and ask these basic questions:

- What's most attractive about this ad, message, colors?
- What action is it asking you to take? And are you compelled to take it?
- Would you buy this product?
- How would you change the ad?
- What's missing?
- What's redundant?
- Is it memorable? Is it forgetful? Is it catchy?
- If you could change one thing, what would it be?

In the case of creating a campaign, if you've been working with a coach, you could bring your ideas to her, and she could give her professional advice. Again, depending on your budget, you might consider consulting with a focus group to decide on the best approach. Stay open to receiving feedback from the group (positive or negative), and make sure to make the adjustments needed. You may also hire a third party to moderate the focus group—this way the participants could be more willing to share their opinions.

You may want to include testimonials in your marketing materials, which also give you another opportunity to talk to your clients to ask for their feedback. Remember to get their permission to include the testimonials on your ads, flyers, website, etc.

Since the business is your baby, and because you understand your mission and values, your clients and your products and services better than anyone else, make sure to share your knowledge with the marketing professional. This is the best way to get a campaign that reflects what your business stands for and to get new or repeat customers.

If you don't have the budget to hire a graphic designer or a marketing professional, do your best to create your own brand, campaign and press releases. Other affordable marketing strategies include blogging, social networking, and networking in person. Your best attempt will be better than no marketing at all.

Financial Help

This book discusses getting help for your business, and finances are one of the main aspects that can determine the success of your business. I recommend that you understand your books. Make sure to keep control of the cash flowing in and out, and to know the real costs of each product or service, otherwise you may not have enough money to keep operating, or to keep promoting the business.

I once helped a client figure out her production costs. Once we compared the time she spent to cook and prepare each product, the cost of the ingredients, how much she was able to produce per hour, and all the production expenses, with the price she planned to charge, it turned out that there would not be much money left to pay her a salary, and that's not even counting the time she would spend promoting and selling her products. It is probably fine to make less money than you anticipate, but you need to know how much you're spending in order to be able to have a plan to increase your earnings.

In the aforementioned case, it was obvious that either the price had to go up, or she had to find ways to reduce production costs. Make sure to either analyze your costs yourself, or work with a business coach to evaluate your expenses.

Once you are aware of the costs of your product or service, the next step is to watch your sales. Cash flow is an important part of your business and, even if you hire a bookkeeper, check it every day or week to make sure that the numbers make sense and are compatible with what's happening in your business: your inventory, your sales, your production.

As a general rule, make sure you are the one signing the company's checks so that you are always in control.

Sales Projections

The sales projections of your business will show a lender that you will be able to pay back the loan, and it will show investors the potential gains on their investments.

In reality, there is no sure way of knowing what your sales will be when launching a new campaign, a new product, a new website or opening a new location. But you can have an idea of the outcomes. You can actually start with the goal in mind.

What's your goal with the new marketing strategy, new location, or new site? Once you can quantify your intentions, then it's time to go back to the drawing board to find out how you are going to get there.

To determine the sales projections, the best thing is to research the data available at the library and research databases, ask others (more than one person is better), and start preparing realistic projections. Some entrepreneurs go further, by preparing three projections: the pessimistic, the realistic and the optimistic one. In order to get to those projections, there is no question that assumptions need to be made, but if you have enough data on hand, you are making an educated guess. Once you keep track of your inventory and sales, for at least a year, it becomes easier to understand each product/service's seasonality, and you can better plan for the following year. Ask for your business coach's assistant to prepare the financials and the projections.

Three steps to eliminating or minimizing guesswork:

- **Conduct secondary research:** Review media kits, research similar businesses, read industry articles, study the market trends.

- **Conduct primary research:** Ask other business owners, ask clients, survey your neighborhood, etc.

- **Study your own capacity and history:** Which strategies have worked in the past, which got the best results, do they still work? How much can you grow at your current capacity? What's your limit today? What would you need to move it forward?

Funding Sources

Before raising funds to grow your business, analyze how financially healthy your business is today—the results could determine your funding options. Don't forget to develop a thorough business plan, and research exactly how much money you need and how much money you have to pursue your growth strategy. Then, it is time to review the self-inquiry exercises in chapter 1 and review the goals you have for your business (if you would want to sell it, franchise it, keep it small, grow it steadily, get partners, give up control, retain control, go public, etc.). Consider if you want to raise funds through loans, through equity investment, through family and friends or invest your own capital. Remember, to the best of your knowledge, to analyze the risks and rewards of each option. Once you have an idea of the best course of action for you, discuss it with your coach, financial advisor, mastermind group or network.

One of the capital sources available is from banks. Here is an outline of the basics for getting a loan from a bank (Keep in mind that each lender has its own criteria and might request additional information):

- **A business plan:** If you've been in business for over two years, there is a possibility that the plan won't be required, you'll only be asked for the company history and tax returns, but it always helps to have one.

- **A three-year financial projection:** The first year should represent monthly projections, and the following two years could be quarterly or yearly estimates. The financial statements include profit and loss statement, income statement, and balance sheet.

- **The business's financial history:** Copies of personal and business tax returns.

- **Capacity:** Banks want to see that your cash flow will facilitate the payback of the loan.

- **Credit/FICO Score:** Good business credit helps, and personal credit is equally important, since anyone who owns 20% or more in the company needs to give a personal guarantee that the loan will be paid. The lender will verify the borrower's credit and payment trends.

- **Collateral:** You will need collateral, and depending on the situation, the equipment or asset you are purchasing could be the collateral.

- **Experience:** At least two years experience is very helpful.

- **Conditions:** The external forces that may affect your business: Industry trends and the social, political and economic environment.

- **Your own money to invest in the business** (Capital infusion or Equity): No bank will fund 100% of your financial needs. Depending on your industry, a bank may ask you to invest 20% to 50% of the capital and share the start-up or expansion costs.

You might be able to get a bank loan even if you don't have all of the above, but it certainly helps. On the other hand, if your credit isn't good, if you have too much debt, no collateral or no experience, it becomes harder to obtain a loan from a bank. The U.S. Small Business Administration (SBA) offers guarantees in certain cases to assist those who might not get a loan otherwise; however, the bank needs to approve the loan first, and SBA wants collateral to make sure they can collect if the business isn't paying the loan. You do have options, though. There are CDFI (Community Development Financial Institutions Fund) agencies serving low-income areas and underserved economically distressed markets, and not-for-profit organizations that offer micro-loans to those who aren't bankable. Some micro-lenders have programs to target women in business and you may be able to benefit from them, if you meet their requirements of income, geographic location, and other criteria they may have.

You can also open a bank account and apply for a loan at a Credit Union in your neighborhood. You need to check each Credit Union's criteria to find out if you qualify. Make sure you understand all the closing fees and interest rates when applying for a loan from banks, micro-lenders, peer-to-peer lending programs, or a Credit Union.

If your personal or business credit is bad, even if you've been in business for a while, and you can't demonstrate a working cash flow, it's not likely that a bank or anyone else will lend you anything. But as you build your business, you might be able to get a smaller loan to make a portion of the changes you want, and grow from there.

Depending on the economic climate, it may be harder for companies to get loans. In tough times, banks may reduce the amount of loans being offered even to those who have good credit and stable growing companies. What do you do when that happens? How do you pursue your goals?

At one of the economic summits I attended, one of the speakers, Patrick J. MacKrell, president and CEO of the New York Business Development Corporation, talked about how to reduce the cost of capital (or rate of interest) when borrowing money from a bank. He suggested that you ask the bank for that reduction. Either ask how it can be reduced now, or if now is not an option, how you can reduce it in the future, so that you can eventually get a better rate. Here are a few questions he suggested to ask the bank:

- What are the factors affecting my cost of capital?
- How did you determine my cost of capital?
- How can I get a lower rate now?
- What can we do today to positively change the rate in the future?

Alternative Sources of Funding

If you don't qualify for a bank loan, and a micro-loan isn't enough (usually from $1,500 up to $30,000 for start-ups, and up to $50,000 for existing businesses), you might consider asking for help from friends and family. Having a business plan and conservative and realistic projections can help you win their trust by showing that you have thought through the plan and you can make it work. But remember to consider those who are not struggling financially, this way you don't have to worry that they'll soon ask for their money back. It is a good idea to also prepare an agreement, explaining how soon you will start paying them back, how much per month, what the interest rate is if any, etc. It is important that your family and friends understand the fact that you will not be able to pay back the loan as soon as you invest the money in the business, and that there are risks. Friends and family are usually more flexible than financial institutions and might allow you to defer making the initial payments by six months or a year. The entire agreement should be clear from the beginning and included in a contract.

If you want to borrow money from friends, family, neighbors or acquaintances, you still need to ask for it. One of the people I mentor informally was excited to share her new business idea with me. She mentioned that she shared her idea with several people, hoping they would offer to invest in it. She told me that they were supportive and showed that they believed in her idea, but no one offered to sponsor it. I asked, "Did you ask anyone to sponsor it?" Her answer was, "Not really." Well, it is rarely the case that people will jump onboard without you asking them to; they might simply not know that you need their financial help. When approaching family, friends and potential investors, create a smart strategy to motivate them to invest in your business and prepare a compelling and clear speech. In addition to potential financial gains, it is important to mention the solutions you are providing and the difference you are making for your clients and/or the community.

You might also consider adding a partner who can provide a cash injection into your business. In this case, look for a partner with the same values and vision, and with complementary skills. The roles and responsibilities of each partner must be defined up front. Don't forget also to write a business agreement, before things are either going great or terrible. Consulting with a business lawyer is key.

Other sources of capital you may consider seeking are equity investment. But before approaching investors, it might be a good idea to ask for help from a financial advisor. She will be able to help you develop an appealing package and reach out to investors. Make sure to ask for referrals from your lawyer, accountant, and/or your networks, check references, and understand the contract and all fees and commissions involved.

Two of the equity investment options available are angel investors and venture capitalists (VCs). Angel investors typically invest a smaller amount than a VC firm, and are usually more willing to invest in start-ups and early stage businesses. Angel investors are individuals, most likely entrepreneurs seeking to share their knowledge, to invest in an industry they have an interest in, and to receive higher returns on their financial investments. If you want to locate angel investors who might be willing to invest in your company, the best thing is to search for angels in your specific industry. They will better understand your business model, and be a source of expertise. According to business expert Michael Wilhite, angel investors are usually able to take on a higher level of risk in their investment strategy. The angel investors' expectations vary, and they might expect returns of 5 to 20 times of invested capital within a five-year period. Mr. Wilhite also warns, "There are no public security exchanges listing "Angel" investment securities so meeting angel investors is tough. You can meet angels through referrals or other business contacts. Being personally introduced to angel investors is the best way to meet them. If you are fortunate you may be able to pitch your business plan in face-to-face meetings or through investor conferences, and competitions."

The National Venture Capital Association describes Venture Capital firms as usually "private partnerships or closely-held corporations funded by private and public pension funds, endowment funds, foundations, corporations, wealthy individuals, foreign investors, and the venture capitalists themselves." The VC investment is possibly harder to get depending on your industry, your company size, how long you've been in business and your growth projections. VCs will be looking for companies with rapid growth potential that can go public, or can merge or be acquired by another company for considerable gains. Investors may also seek to have management control.

When approaching equity investors, make sure to have your elevator pitch ready, which explains your value proposition, your well-written business plan with a concise and thorough executive summary, and realistic financial projections. Investors want to see that you have a great management team in place and that you can show a successful business track record. You can conduct your own valuation studies to determine the value of your company, although the investors will do due diligence before investing.

If you are considering raising funds through equity financing, the resources chapter provides references to help with your research. One of the resources is the company Springboard Enterprises, which offers programs, events and training for women business owners seeking equity investment.

"Springboard educates, showcases and supports women entrepreneurs as they seek capital and build their businesses." To learn more, visit www.springboardenterprises.org.

Don't forget to ask for help in valuating your business and making sure the numbers make sense, to ask for VC and angel referrals, to take into consideration all the potential risks involved, to review your own goals and vision for your business and lifestyle, and to ask your business lawyer to review all documents.

If you are declined a loan or can't get equity investment the first time you try, listen to the feedback you receive, make the suggested changes, go back to the lenders or investors if they give you the option, or look for other organizations that might be interested in investing in your business. Although the negative response might be discouraging, remember to research other options, make adjustments and keep going.

When none of the aforementioned options are available or possible to reach, you can still brainstorm creative ways of achieving your financial needs. You could have a raffle, you could create sponsorship opportunities on your website, you could host a fundraising event, you could participate in a business plan competition, you could negotiate better payment terms with your suppliers, you could brainstorm creative alternatives and you could barter the services you need.

Bartering Services

No matter what your financial situation is today, it is always possible to move your business forward. You can work on a plan of action; you can take a part-time job to learn/develop a particular skill that you might need for your business; you might find free and useful tools online; you can take classes and you can barter services. Even if you are ready to take a certain course, but you're short on the money you can consider asking to volunteer, asking to pay the fee in installments, or asking to get a scholarship. Rather than looking at the price and feeling defeated, consider reaching out to the host of the event. You could offer to refer a few people and get your spot for free or you could barter your services for the course. I'm sure you can come up with creative ways of getting where you want to be.

I have bartered coaching services with other coaches. It was an easy exchange: during a one-hour call, we each got 30 minutes to devote to solving our own issues. You don't need to be a coach to barter products or services though. I know of a business that bartered gift baskets in exchange for billboard ads for example.

A photographer might offer to take pictures of an event for free in exchange for her name being mentioned in the program, in all marketing materials, and for the photos being posted with a blurb about her. The same goes for a caterer starting out. When you are the one offering the free service, make sure that you can safely budget it into your business plan. If not, you could offer a discount but charge an amount that would at least cover your costs. Plan wisely, so that you will have sales by the end of the event. Always remember to ask your accountant about the tax implications and the correct procedures of bartering products and services.

There are other areas in your business that you might need help with, such as the day-to-day operations of your business, the management, the taxes issues, the legal aspects, the technology needs, and issues specific to your own industry. The specific ones I discussed: business planning, marketing and advertising, and finances give you the basic tools and opportunities to ask for help with other specific challenges your business could face.

CONCLUSION/FINAL THOUGHTS

Let Go of Perfectionism

You probably know by now that one of the main obstacles to our success is our own self. We get in the way of what can sometimes be simple tasks. The thinking goes, "It has to be perfect, it has to be this way or no way, it has to happen as I envision it." When our idea doesn't go as planned, which is pretty much all the time, we get disappointed, blame ourselves and others, and we might end up getting stuck.

For me, writing this book was hard for this reason. I had to make a difference in every line, I had to offer a new way of looking at things in every paragraph, and I had to make it profound for all readers. Until I let go of the ideal, I couldn't allow myself to finish the book. What's holding you back?

Take a look at your own situation right now and ask yourself:

- What is it that isn't happening the way I envisioned?
- What are other ways that I could make my business, vision, and dream happen?
- What do I need to let go?
- How can I let go of this long time dream? Could I just let go of the desire for perfection and still accomplish my goal another way?
- In what other ways would I be satisfied if this vision didn't happen?
- How am I trying to be perfect? How can I let go of this need?

Awareness of your patterns is half the battle. The next step is to slowly let go of control, and allow things to happen. Of course, this doesn't mean that you should stop taking action toward achieving your goals; it just means that whatever happens won't stop you from finding a solution to get you closer to your dream.

Being flexible in your personal relationships, professional encounters and business situations is mandatory for your own sanity and survival. If you try to be perfect and to control everything and everyone, the amount of energy spent and stress felt is draining and overwhelming. Face every situation with this thought in mind: "Everything will work out the way it is meant to be." By being focused, you will achieve success faster than you otherwise could have. In addition, when you give yourself permission to look past perfection, you can see that your current situation is better than anything that could have happened otherwise.

Support

As you build your business, having a support group and like-minded advisors makes all the difference. When I started WomenandBiz.com I had two people who believed in me and were my cheerleaders, but I had to find volunteers to help create content and through the years other professionals have helped me. During a career transition, I worked with a coach, but I also practiced meditation, I wrote a journal, and I had friends who were supportive and understanding.

Before asking for help, my recommendation is that you start from within. Ask yourself the questions mentioned in chapter 1, and then ask for referrals for a coach or join an organization, or create a mastermind group. Equally important is to find something to help you take your mind off the situation, such as a sport or a hobby.

When asking for help make sure to trust your instincts, and when in doubt, ask for guidance from the Universe and from within. Through meditation, quiet moments, or by taking your mind off of the problem and coming back to it later on, it is more likely that the best solutions and actions will come to you.

If you have someone in mind whom can help you and you are unable to reach her for whatever reason, or if she is not available, don't spend time being stuck. Start asking for referrals right away. When seeking support from friends, keep in mind that at times they might not be your best supporters, and you can ask for help from someone else.

Remember, don't try to change every aspect of your life and business all at once. I wish I could say this was possible, but I really don't think it is. Sometimes you need to take time, accept your business as it is, and focus more energy on your relationships. You might need to take some extra time to heal a relationship that you let go, you might need time to figure out which relationships to let go, or your family might need your full attention. It's definitely important to aim for a fully balanced life, but know that it might take time to achieve it. Deep inside you know that there is always work to be done in one area of your life or another. Just make sure to prioritize what to take care of first. Please be kind to yourself and be there for yourself at all times.

Know When to Stop Asking

How much help does a person need? The answer varies. Depending on the stage of your life and business, you might need all the help you can get, or just one person with the right answer will do. When do you stop asking? When you haven't taken a step for a long time. When you keep asking and asking and asking, but you don't actually go for it and find out if it's possible to achieve anything. At some point you have to take action. Any action–one step!

What could you do today? Could you follow one piece of advice you received? Could you follow your intuition? Sometimes the action is as simple as downloading a free trial of a bookkeeping system. Other times, it might mean that in order to really follow what you know you are supposed to do, you might need to take classes. Be it business, art, technology, self-development, accounting, business writing, or any skill that could be crucial to your personal and professional success. Or it could mean actually taking the leap and reinventing your business or getting investors.

Trust Yourself

Even with all the tools in this book and in many other books out there, it is still always up to you to choose the right ones for you and your business. After coaching hundreds of individuals I can say that there have never been two people with the same idea and the same method for executing it.

Not following standard rules developed by someone else means being free to be yourself, and as long as you are honoring your own self and your own guidance, your business will be unique.

Through the process of seeking professional advice and asking for help in any area of your business, the key is to listen to your heart, attune yourself to your own intuition, make a decision, take action and trust yourself through it all.

The only way to master asking for help is by doing it, but make sure to ask yourself first and last, trust your instincts and don't forget to ask for referrals before hiring someone.

Cheers to your continued success and to the achievement of your dreams!

Appendix: Suggested Reading and Resources

For an updated list, visit <u>www.askotherstrustyourself.com</u>.

Self-improvement and Inspiration

The 7 Habits of Highly Effective People, by Stephen R. Covey. New York, NY: Free Press (A Division of Simon & Schuster, Inc.), 2004. Copyright 1989, 2004 by Stephen R. Covey.

Embracing your Inner Critic: Turning Self-Criticism into a Creative Asset, by Hal Stone and Sidra Stone. San Francisco, CA: HarperOne, 1993.

The Seeker's Guide: Making Your Life a Spiritual Adventure, by Elizabeth Lesser. New York, NY: Villard Books, 1999.

The Art of Possibility: Transforming Professional and Personal Life, by Rosamund Stone Zander and Benjamin Zander. New

York, NY: Penguin Books, 2002. First published in the United States of America by Harvard Business School Press 2000, published in Penguin Books 2002.

Stand Up For Your Life: A Practical Step-By-Step Plan to Build Inner Confidence and Personal Power, by Cheryl Richardson. New York, NY: Free Press, 2002.

Ask and It Is Given: Learning to Manifest Your Desires, by Esther and Jerry Hicks. Carlsbad, CA: Hay House, 2004.

The Success Principles: How to Get from Where You Are to Where You Want to Be, by Jack Canfield with Janet Switzer. New York, NY: HarperCollins Publishers, 2005.

More Than 85 Broads: Women Making Career Choices, Taking Risks, and Defining Success—On Their Own Terms, by Janet Hanson. New York, NY: McGraw-Hill, 2006.

Business

Permission Marketing: Turning Strangers Into Friends, And Friends Into Customers, by Seth Godin. New York, NY: Simon & Schuster, 1999.

Cold Calling for Women: Opening Doors & Closing Sales, by Wendy Weiss. New York, NY: D.F.D. Publications Inc., 2000.

Blue Ocean Strategy: How to Create Uncontested Market Space and Make the Competition Irrelevant, by W. Chan Kim and Renée Mauborgne. Boston, MA: Harvard Business School Publishing Corporation, 2005.

The Girl's Guide to Getting on Top: Positioning Your Business Through Media Placements, by Laurel Tielis. New York, NY: Somerset House, 2006.

Savvy Networking: 118 Fast & Effective Tips for Business Success, by Andrea Nierenberg. Sterling, VA: Capital Books, 2007

Bankable Business Plans: Second Edition, by Edward G. Rogoff. New York, NY: Rowhouse Publishing, 2007.

Elisa Balabram

The Girls' Guide to Building a Million-Dollar Business, by
Susan Wilson Solovic. New York, NY: AMACOM, 2008.
.

DVDs

The Dream Giver. By Bruce Wilkinson. Actor: Bruce
Wilkinson. Good Times Video, 2004.

What the Bleep Do We Know!? Writers: Betsy Chasse, Mark
Vicente, William Arntz, Matthew Hoffman. Prod. Betsy
Chasse. Dir. Betsy Chasse, Mark Vicente, William Arntz. Perf.
Marlee Matlin, Elaine Hendrix, John Ross Bowie, Robert
Bailey Jr., Barry Newman. 20th Century Fox, 2005.

Resources

WomenandBiz: Author's online magazine for women
entrepreneurs and aspiring business owners. It contains
information about woman-owned businesses, marketing, sales
and networking tips, and resources to help women start and

178

grow their businesses. Subscribe for free at:
www.womenandbiz.com

U.S. Small Business Administration (SBA) - It includes resources, services and online training for small business owners, as well as a list of all resource partners nationwide (WBC, SBDC and SCORE): ww.sba.gov

SBA Women's Business Centers - Visit the website to locate the center near you: www.sba.gov/women

Internal Revenue Service – Tax information for businesses: www.irs.gov/businesses

U.S. Patent and Trademark Office Home Page: www.uspto.gov

Census Bureau: www.Census.gov

Small Business Center - New York Public Library: http://smallbiz.nypl.org

SBDCNet - National SBDC Information Clearing House: www.sbdcnet.org

Advisory Guides to Business Law by Nina Kaufman, Esq.:
http://www.greatbusinesslawtips.com

Women's Business Enterprise National Council – The largest
third-party certifier of businesses owned and operated by
women in the United States: www.wbenc.org

Center for Women's Business Research:
www.womensbusinessresearchcenter.org

Make Mine a $Million Business – Started in 2005 by Count Me
In For Women's Economic Independence with founding partner
OPEN from American Express®, Make Mine a $Million
Business program offers money, business resources, mentoring,
marketing and technology tools for women. For more
information visit: www.makemineamillion.org

Equity Financing

Angel Capital Education
Foundation: www.angelcapitaleducation.org

Angelsoft Network: http://angelsoft.net

National Venture Capital Association: www.nvca.org

SBA Small Business Investment Company program:
http://www.sba.gov/inv

Springboard Enterprises: www.springboardenterprises.org

Associations

Women President's Organization:
www.womenpresidentsorg.com

National Association of Women Business Owners:
www.NAWBO.org

National Association of Female Executives: www.NAFE.com

Women's eCommerce Association, International™:
www.wecai.org

About the Author

Elisa Balabram is the founder and editor of WomenandBiz.com, an online magazine for women business owners established in 2003. She is a writer, business coach and speaker and was named the U.S. Small Business Administration New York District 2008 Women in Business Champion of the Year, "For significant contributions to, and dedicated support of, small businesses." Prior to moving to New York, Elisa Balabram assisted in running her family's business (Coffee shop and chocolate business) in Brazil. She holds an MBA in Entrepreneurship Management from Zicklin School of Business at Baruch College, CUNY, and a Bachelor's degree in Civil Engineering.

LaVergne, TN USA
10 March 2011
219511LV00001B/2/P